Emanuel Hecht

Biblical History for Israelitish Schools

Edition VII

Emanuel Hecht

Biblical History for Israelitish Schools
Edition VII

ISBN/EAN: 9783337101671

Printed in Europe, USA, Canada, Australia, Japan

Cover: Foto ©Lupo / pixelio.de

More available books at **www.hansebooks.com**

BIBLICAL HISTORY

FOR

ISRAELITISH SCHOOLS,

WITH A BRIEF OUTLINE OF THE

Geography of Palestine.

BY EMANUEL HECHT.

REVISED AND CORRECTED

BY DR. S. ADLER,

RABBI AND PREACHER OF THE CONGREGATION EMANU-EL, NEW YORK,

TRANSLATED FROM THE GERMAN

BY DR. M. MAYER.

VII EDITION.

NEW-YORK:
PUBLISHED AND FOR SALE BY M. THALMESSINGER & Co.,
PRINTERS AND STATIONERS, 337 BROADWAY.

1874.

PRIMEVAL HISTORY OF THE HUMAN RACE

1. THE CREATION OF THE WORLD. [Genesis i.]

THERE was a time when nothing existed except God Himself, the Everlasting and Uncreated Being. He created everything—whatever is above and around us—all that is in heaven and upon earth, *from nothing*, merely through His will. God proclaimed: "Let there be!" and upon this command the whole universe sprang into existence. On the first day, God said: "Let there be light!" and there was light. On the *second* day, God created the *heaven*, the blue expanse above us. On the *third* day, God caused the *dry land* to appear, and made the ocean, the fountains, the brooks and rivers, and the flowers, grasses, and herbs. On the *fourth* day, God created the *sun*, the *moon*, and the *stars*. On the *fifth* day, His creative power produced the *fishes* in the water, and the *birds* in the air. On the *sixth* day, God created the *creeping animals*, *cattle*, and the *beasts* of the field; and at last, when the universe had been finished in its beauty and wise order, He created *man*, after His own image, and thus made him the master-piece among all created beings on earth.*

---

* The following verses may assist the memory of the pupils in studying the history of the Creation:

The *first* creation-day God said: "Let there be light!"
The *second* did behold the vault of heaven bright;
The *third*, He made the brooks, trees, ocean, flowers fair.

God made man in the following manner. He formed a beautiful human body of dust from the ground. But this body was yet without motion and life. He, therefore, breathed the breath of life, a spirit from His own spirit into it. And thus the first man, who received the name of *Adam*, meaning: Man of Earth, sprang into existence. And God said: "It is not good that the man should be alone: I will make him a help suitable for him." A deep sleep fell upon Adam, and God took one of his ribs, while he was asleep, and formed it into a woman, and Adam called her *Eve*, (חַוָּה,) that is, Mother of all Living. These first human beings are our progenitors, and the progenitors of all men. On the *seventh* day, God rested from all His works, that is to say, He ceased from creating—and commanded that we also should rest from all our labors, on the Sabbath, remember God and His creation, and offer up to him our thanksgivings, for His love and goodness.

---

§ 2. The First Sin. [Genesis ii. iii.]

God planted a pleasant garden, called *Gan Eden*, or *Paradise*, and appointed it to be the dwelling place of Adam and Eve. In this garden there stood all kinds of fruit-trees, pleasant to the sight and good for food. And God commanded the man, saying: "Of every tree of the garden thou mayest eat; but of the tree of the knowledge of good and evil, thou shalt not eat of it; for as soon as thou eatest thereof thou shalt die." God did not intend, by this prohibition, to mar the joys of our first parents, but willed only that they should always be obedient to Him, believe in His word, follow His commands, and love Him above all things. But they soon transgressed the command of God, and sinned. This happened in the

---

The *fourth* He bade the sun, and moon, and stars appear;
The fishes on the *fifth*, and birds began to be,
And on the *sixth*, the world the beasts and *man* did see.

following manner. Once Eve approached the tree of the forbidden fruit. On the tree there was a serpent, that addressed her thus: "Do not believe that you must die as soon as you have eaten of the fruit of this tree; do but eat, and you will then become wise, and be able to know good from evil, and be like unto God Himself." Eve believed more in the tempting words of the serpent than the command of God. She now contemplated the fruit of the tree still more attentively, and observed that it was good for food and pleasant to the eyes. Her desire to taste of it grew stronger within her heart. She took of it, did eat, and gave also to her husband, and he also did eat. And thus the first sin was committed. But their sin of disobedience was soon followed by punishment. Their eyes were opened, they now knew that they had done wrong, and were able to discern the evil from the good which they could have fulfilled. They felt profound *grief* in their hearts, on account of their sin; they were ashamed, became afraid, and hid themselves from the face of God. But God, who sees, hears, and knows everything, perceived also their sin, and said: "Adam, where art thou?" And Adam answered: "I heard Thy voice, and I was afraid because I was naked, and therefore I hid myself." And God said: "Who told thee that thou art naked? Hast thou eaten of the fruit whereof I commanded thee that thou shouldest not eat?" Whereupon Adam said: "The woman whom Thou gavest to be with me, gave me of the fruit, and I did eat." And God said: "*Eve*, why hast thou done this?" And she answered: "The serpent beguiled me, and I did eat." Then God said unto the serpent: "Because thou hast beguiled the weak woman by *sneaking* hypocrisy, thou shalt be cursed above all cattle, and above every beast of the field; upon thy belly shalt thou *creep*, and dust shalt thou eat all the days of thy life." Unto Eve He said: "Because thou hast *obeyed* the serpent *rather* than the word of God, obedience shall henceforth be thy lot. Thy husband shall rule over thee, and in sorrow shalt thou train children." And unto Adam he said: "Since thou hast suffered *pleasures of the senses* to mislead thee, thy earthly enjoyments shall henceforth cause thee trouble. With great labor shalt thou till the

ground, and in the sweat of thy face shalt thou eat thy
bread, until thou shalt return unto the ground whence
thou wast taken; *for dust thou art, and unto dust shalt
thou return.*"
God then drove them from Paradise, and placed the
cherubim with the flaming sword at the east of the garden
to keep the way of the tree of life.

----

§ 3. CAIN AND ABEL. [Genesis iv.]

(*Kayin and Habel.*)

Adam and Eve had two sons; the elder was named
Cain, (Kayin,) the younger *Abel*, (Habel). Cain was a
tiller of the ground, and Abel a keeper of sheep; the
former was of a haughty disposition, while the latter was
meek and pious. Now, both offered sacrifices before
God; Cain offered of the fruit of the ground, and Abel
the *best* of his flock. When Cain saw that God's blessing
rested upon his brother, and that his offering was favorably
accepted, he became exceedingly wroth, so that his inward
anger was very manifest. And God said to Cain: "Why
is thy countenance fallen? Behold if thou art pious, thou
also shalt be accepted; and if thou art not pious, sin
lurketh before thy door, and unto thee is its desire, but
thou canst conquer it." But Cain paid no attention to
God's paternal admonition; his heart hardened more and
more, and he said once to his brother: "Come, let us go
into the field." When they were far away from their
home and parents, the revengeful Cain rose up against
his brother, and slew him. But severe were the pangs of
conscience within Cain's bosom after he had perpetrated
the atrocious fratricide; he enjoyed neither rest nor ease.
And God said unto him: "Where is Abel, thy brother?"
Cain answered: "I know not! Am I my brother's
keeper?" But God said: "What hast thou done? The
voice of thy brother's blood crieth unto me from the
ground. Cursed be for thee, therefore, the ground which
hath opened its mouth to receive thy brother's blood; as

a fugitive and vagabond shalt thou wander about upon earth, and nowhere find rest and repose." Then said Cain unto the Eternal: "My guilt is too heavy for me to bear. Behold, Thou hast driven me away this day from this ground, and from Thy face must I hide myself; a fugitive I must be upon the earth, and every one that finds me shall slay me." But God said: "Whosoever slays Cain, vengeance shall be taken on him sevenfold." The conscience-stricken Cain then removed from the land which he had defiled with his brother's blood, and fled to the country of Nod, on the east of Eden. Such was the realization of the joy and comfort which the poor parents of Cain and Abel had hoped to receive at the hands of their children. But God had compassion upon Adam and Eve, and gave them another son, who was named Sheth. At the time of Enosh, the son of Sheth, men began to call upon God, and Enoch, a later descendant of Sheth's led a pious, godly life, and God took him soon to Himself. All men reached, at those early times, a very old age; Methushelah, the length of whose life exceeded that of all other men, lived 969 years. His son was Lemech, and the son of the latter, Noah.

_____

§ 4. NOAH. [Genesis vi.] 1656 A.M.

Men gradually multiplied upon the face of the earth; but they grew more and more corrupt, and committed many godless deeds. Even the descendants of the pious were led away from the path of virtue by the examples of the wicked. They married the daughters of the latter, and soon became, like these, corrupt and godless. But few believed that there was a God in heaven who saw and knew every thing. Noah and his wife alone remained pious, and would not suffer themselves to be led astray by their wicked fellow-men. They guarded their children also—as is the duty of good parents—against the evil influence and corruption of their age, as much as it lay in their power.

And God said to Noah : "The end of all flesh is come before me, for the earth is full of violence. But thou, go and make thee an ark, 300 cubits long, 50 broad, and 30 high. For behold, I shall bring a flood of waters upon the earth, to destroy all flesh, wherein is the breath of life. Every thing that is on earth shall die. But with thee I will establish my covenant; and thou shalt come into the ark, thou and thy sons, *Sem, Ham, and Japhet,* and thy wife, and thy sons' wives with thee. Take with thee also provisions of food, and of all sorts of animals that can not exist in water; of every clean beast thou shalt take with thee seven pair, and of beasts that are not clean take one pair, to keep seed alive upon the earth after the flood." And Noah did as God had commanded him. Hereupon all the fountains of the earth opened, and rain poured down from heaven forty days and forty nights. The waters increased more and more, and became at last so high, that even the tops of the highest mountains were covered. All living creatures were destroyed, man, cattle, birds, and creeping animals; only Noah and they that were with him in the ark, were saved alive.

§ 5. Noah's Departure from the Ark.

One hundred and fifty days the waters prevailed upon the earth. And God remembered Noah, and every living being, and the cattle that dwelt with him in the ark, and caused a wind to pass over the earth, that the waters of the deep and the windows of heaven were stopped; the rain ceased, the waters subsided, and the ark rested upon the mountain *Ararat,* and the tops of the mountains gradually rose again above the waters.

Noah, after some time, opened a window of the ark and sent forth a raven, to see whether the water had sufficiently fallen or not. But the raven, having no doubt found food upon the mountain, flew to and fro, and then never returned. After some time, Noah sent forth a dove, which returned to the ark, because it could find no place to rest upon on account of the waters that were still on the earth.

After waiting seven days, he sent forth the dove a second time. Toward evening she returned again, but this time with an olive leaf in her mouth, by which joyful token Noah perceived that the waters had abated, But he waited seven more days, after the lapse of which he sent forth the dove for the third time. But she returned no more, so that Noah knew that the waters were dried from the earth.

Now God said unto Noah: "Go forth from the ark, thou, and thy wife, and thy sons, and the wives of thy sons, with thee, and all living creatures." And Noah went forth from the ark, together with all living beings. The first thing which he then did, was to thank God for his deliverance. He built an altar, and, according to the custom of his time, offered a sacrifice upon it. This act of gratitude pleased God so much, that He said: "I will not again curse the earth any more for man's sake, although the imagination of man's heart is evil from his youth; neither will I smite any more every thing living as I have now done." And He blessed Noah and his sons, and said unto them: "Behold, I establish my covenant with you, and with your descendants; I shall not again send a flood upon the earth, nor shall the order of the universe be disturbed any more. While the earth remains, seed-time and harvest, and cold and heat, and summer and winter, and day and night shall not cease." At this moment, when Noah raised his eyes towards the sky, he beheld a rainbow with its soft brightness and majesty in the clouds. And God said: "This rainbow shall be for a token and pledge of my covenant, and of my mercy wherewith I look down upon the earth. But follow ye also my commandments; ye may rule over all the beasts of the earth, and every moving thing that liveth shall be meat for you; but ye shall not eat the flesh thereof as long as there is life in it. Whoso sheddeth man's blood, by man shall his blood be shed; for in the image of God made He man. But ye, be ye fruitful and multiply."

Noah again tilled the ground, and discovered the vine, and improved and cultivated it. But not knowing the great power of wine, he drank too much of it, became intoxicated, and lay *uncovered* in his tent. How heinous a vice is *drunkenness!* His son Ham saw him, and laughed at him scornfully. But his other two sons, Sem and Japhet, who were more respectful children, covered him in a most delicate manner. When Noah awoke and heard of the rude conduct of Ham, he punished him, but blessed and praised Sem and Japhet, and appointed them to rule over their unfeeling brother. God also punished Ham and blessed his brothers.

----

§ 6. The Descendants of Noah. [Genesis x. xi.]

The sons of Noah now became the progenitors of the human race. The number of their descendants gradually increased; but the more they multiplied, the more extensive pastures they required for their flocks, and the more room for themselves; so that they were compelled to separate from each other. Now, as this was not agreeable to them, they resolved to build a tower that should reach to heaven, in order that it might be visible to all, and serve them for a place from which they could be speedily called together, whenever it was necessary. They immediately set to work, burned bricks and prepared mortar, and began the building; but forgot God, without whose blessing nothing can be accomplished. On this account, God scattered and dispersed them, that in consequence at last, they could not understand each other's speech. The place where they intended to erect the tower, received in memory of this event, the name of Babel (*confusion*.) They were compelled to desist from their work, and spread over the earth. There are every where good and beautiful things ordained by Divine Providence to be enjoyed by man. For this reason the human race was scattered, that they should behold every where the glorious works of God, and employ them for their own purposes. But whatever He wills, man can not change.

II.

THE PATRIARCHS.

——o——

§ 7 ABRAHAM, THE PROGENITOR OF THE ISRAELITISH NATION [Genesis xii] 2000 A.M

Terah, one of *Shem's* descendants, lived in *Ur of the Chaldees,* and had three sons, *Abram, Nahor,* and *Haran.* After the death of Haran, Terah took his sons, *Nahor* and *Abram, Sarai,* the wife of the latter, and *Lot,* the son of Haran, and moved to the city of *Haran,* in the land of Mesopotamia, and made it his dwelling-place. Terah and his family, like all their countrymen, did not know the true God; instead of worshipping Him, they worshipped the sun, moon and stars, images and animals. But *Abram* knew how foolish and wrong it was to pay that adoration to created beings, which we owe to God alone. He therefore placed his entire confidence in God alone, and manifested true piety, while all his fellow-men, in his time, were more or less wicked. On this account, God looked with special favor upon him, and cared for him with true paternal kindness; nay, He even conversed with him very often to make known His holy will to him. Once God said to Abram: "Get thee out of thy country, and from thy father's house, and from thy kindred, unto a land which I will show thee. And I will make of thee a great and distinguished nation, *and through thee shall all the generations of the earth be blessed."* At first, this promise did not appear to be followed by its fulfilment; for Abram had no children. Yet Abram knew that whatever God promised would be fulfilled. Therefore, he firmly believed in the word of God, left all those that were dear and near to him, and went with his wife Sarai and his nephew Lot to the land of Canaan. When he reached the city of

Sichem, the Lord appeared to him and promised that his descendants should possess this land, Abram continued his pastoral life, moved about in the country, built altars unto the Lord in various places, and proclaimed, wherever he sojourned, the name of the Almighty.

---

§ 8. ABRAM SHOWING HIS PEACEFUL DISPOSITION AND HIS GENEROSITY. [Genesis xiii. xiv.]

Abram grew very rich in cattle, in silver, and in gold. And Lot also, who went with Abram, had flocks, and herds, and tents. They themselves lived in peace, as it becomes relatives, but their herdmen began to quarrel. Abram therefore said to Lot: "Let there be no strife, I pray thee, between me and thee, and between my herdmen and thy herdmen, for we are brethren! Let us rather separate; choose thou whither thou wishest to move, and I will be satisfied. If thou wilt take the left hand, then I will go to the right, or if thou depart to the right hand, then I will go to the left." Lot chose the region of Sodom, and removed there: but Abram remained in the land of Canaan. It is true, the country which Lot chose for himself was beautiful and fertile, but its inhabitants were very wicked; therefore, his selection was not a good one. Besides, a war soon broke out in that country. *Chadorlaomer*, king of Elam, together with some other kings, with whom he had concluded an alliance, defeated the king of Sodom, plundered the city and the country around, and took men, and beasts, and all their substance with them, as booty. They took also Lot, and his goods, and departed. When Abram heard this, he armed his servants, three hundred and eighteen in number, pursued the conquerors, took them by surprise by night, defeated them, delivered Lot, the women, and the people from the hands of the enemy, and brought back all the goods. On his return, *Melchizedek* (who was a priest of the Most High), went forth to meet him, and brought bread and wine, and said: "Blessed be thou, Abram, of the most high God, possessor of heaven and earth; and blessed be the most high God, who has delivered thy enemies into thy hands." Abram gave him tithes of all. Also the king of Sodom came, and said to Abram: "Give me only the persons, and the goods take to thyself." Then answered Abram: "I have lifted up my hand (for an oath) unto the Eternal, the most high God, the possessor of heaven and earth, that I will not take even a thread or a shoe-latchet, of all that is thine, lest thou shouldest say, I have made Abram rich. Only that which the servants have eaten, and the portion of the men which went with me, Aner, Eshcol and Mamre, let them take their portion."

Thus acts a generous man.

---

§ 9   ABRAHAM, THE MAN OF FAITH. [Genesis xv. xvi.]

Abram was still without children, when God appeared to him and said: "Fear not, Abram, I am thy shield, and exceedingly great shall be thy reward." And Abram answered: "Lord! for what purpose wilt thou give me, seeing that I have no children, and that strangers shall be my heirs?" Hereupon God brought him forth abroad, and said: "Look toward heaven; numberless as the stars shall be thy posterity." And Abram believed God, and He counted it to him for righteousness.

On the same day, God made a covenant with Abram, that his posterity should inherit the land of Canaan.

Shortly afterwards, *Hager* bore a child unto Abram, when he was eighty-six years of age; and Abram called his son *Ishmael*.

When Abram was ninety-nine years old, God appeared again unto him, and said: "I am God, the Almighty; walk before me, and be thou pious." When Abram heard these words he fell on his face, and God continued, saying: "Behold! thou shalt be the father of many nations, and kings shall be among thy descendants. Therefore, thy name shall no longer be called *Abram*, but it shall henceforth be ABRAHAM, (that is, father of a great multitude,)

Sarai shall bear thee a son, and thou shalt no longer call
her *Sarai*, but SARAH shall her name be. Then Abraham
fell upon his face, and laughed for joy, and said within his
heart: "Shall a child be born unto him that is a hundred
years old? and shall Sarah, who is ninety years old, bear?
Oh! that Ishmael might live before Thee!" And God
said: "Surely thy wife Sarah shall bear thee a son indeed;
and thou shalt call his name *Isaac*, (*son of joy*,) and with
him and his posterity I shall establish my covenant. And
concerning Ishmael also, I have heard thee; I shall bless
him and make him a great nation."

---

§ 10. ABRAHAM, THE HOSPITABLE AND COMPASSIONATE PATRIARCH. [Genesis xviii.]

One day, Abraham sat in the tent-door, in the heat of
the day, and saw three strangers in the street. As soon
as he observed them, he ran to meet them, bowed before
them to the ground, and addressed one of them, saying:
"My Lord, if I have found favor in thy sight, pass not
away, I pray thee, from thy servant. Let a little water,
I pray you, be brought, and wash your feet. Then ye
may rest under yonder tree, until I shall bring a morsel
of bread; and when ye shall have refreshed yourselves,
ye may pass on your way." The strangers consented,
and Abraham hastened into his tent, and said to Sarah:
"Quickly bake some cakes." Then he ran to the herd,
selected the finest calf, gave it to a young man that he
might dress it, took butter and milk, set the dishes before
his guests, and remained with them under the tree while
they were eating. One of the strangers asked him:
"Where is Sarah thy wife? · Abraham answered: "She
is in the tent." And the stranger continued, saying:
"One year hence, at this time, I shall return, and Sarah,
thy wife, shall then have a son." Sarah, overhearing these
words, doubted their truth, and smiled secretly. But the
stranger said: "Is any thing impossible for God? Thou
shalt indeed have a son." When the three men had finished
their meal, they rose, and wended their way towards

Sodom; and Abraham went with them to bring them on the way.

Then God said in His heart: "How could I hide aught from Abraham that I shall do? For I know that he will command his children, and his household after him, to do what is right and good." "Know then," said God to Abraham, "that I shall destroy Sodom and Gomorrah, on account of their great and manifold sins." This information caused profound grief in the bosom of the kind-hearted and compassionate Abraham. He could not forbear to plead the cause of the condemned cities before God. "Wilt Thou also destroy the righteous with the wicked?" he asked God. "Perhaps there are fifty righteous within the city: wilt Thou also destroy and not spare the place for the fifty righteous that are therein? Oh! be it far from Thee to do after this manner, to slay the righteous with the wicked, and that the righteous should be as the wicked in Thine eyes. Thou canst not judge thus, who art the Judge of all the earth." God answered: "If I find in Sodom fifty righteous within the city, then I will spare the place for their sakes." Abraham continued to plead for the doomed cities, and said: "Behold now, I have taken upon me to speak unto my Lord, although I am but dust and ashes. Perhaps there shall lack five of the fifty righteous." And God said: "If I find there forty and five, the place shall not be destroyed." Abraham continued, saying: "Perhaps there are but forty righteous in the city." Whereupon God answered: "I will not destroy it for the forty's sake." Abraham then said: "Oh! be not angry my Lord, that I still continue to speak: peradventure there shall thirty be found there." And God answered: "I will spare the city, if I find thirty there." Abraham continued: "Peradventure there shall be twenty found there." And God said: "I will not destroy it for twenty's sake." Abraham answered once more; "O Lord! be not angry, and I will speak yet but this once. Peradventure ten shall be found there." And God said: "I will not destroy it for the ten's sake." Now Abraham continued no longer, but returned to his dwelling-place.

§ 11. The Destruction of Sodom and Gomorrah. [Genesis xix.]

Lot sat in the gate of the city, when, towards evening, the strangers arrived at Sodom. As soon as he saw them, he went to meet them, greeted them, and addressed them with the following words: "Behold now, my lords, turn in, I pray you, into your servant's house, and tarry all night." After many urgent requests on his part, they yielded and went into his house, where he made them a feast. No sooner had the inhabitants of the city heard that strangers had arrived, than they gathered together to insult them. Lot remonstrated with them, but in vain. Already they were about to break the door, when they were struck with blindness; so that they could not even find the door. Hereupon the strangers said to Lot: "Hasten to save thyself with all thy kindred, for we have been sent by God to destroy this wicked city." When the morning arose, and Lot still lingered, the strangers laid hold upon his hand, upon the hand of his wife, and upon the hand of his two daughters, and carried them out of the city. Here they left them, addressing Lot in these words: "Escape for thy life; do not stay to look behind thee, but flee into the mountain, lest thou perish. "Now, an awful storm rose above the cities of Sodom and Gomorrah; they were destroyed and all their inhabitants perished. Lot's wife, who, led by curiosity, had looked behind her, against the orders of the strangers, was changed into a pillar of salt. On the following day, Abraham got up early in the morning to learn what had become of the doomed cities, when the rising clouds of smoke showed him only the place where they had stood. The Dead Sea now occupies the site which the destroyed cities once occupied.

---

§ 12. Abraham's Obedience. [Genesis xxii.]

God fulfilled his promise, and gave Abraham a son. And Abraham named him Isaac. When Isaac had grown older, he was often mocked by his brother Ishmael. For this reason, Sarah could not tolerate the latter, and requested Abraham to send him away with his mother. Abraham was unwilling to comply, but God commanded him to hearken unto Sarah; whereupon he provided Ishmael and Hagar with bread and water, and sent them away. Hagar wandered into the wilderness, and went astray. The water in the bottle was exhausted before she could find another supply. Ishmael was seized by the most burning thirst, and yet she could find no fountain whence to satisfy and thus to save her son. She then placed him under one of the shrubs, and said: "I can not see the child die." She wept and prayed to God, and God heard her. An angel appeared, and showed her a well of water, from which she filled her bottle, and gave her child to drink. God was also in future with Ishmael, and made him the progenitor of a great nation, which numbers twelve tribes, called the ISHMAELITES.

After some time, God tried Abraham, and said to him: "Take now thy son, thine only son Isaac, whom thou lovest, go with him into the land of Moriah, and offer him there for a sacrifice upon one of the mountains which I will tell thee of." Abraham obeyed. He rose up early in the morning, took two of his servants and his son Isaac with him, went unto the mountain of which God had told him, built an altar, laid the wood on it, and then his son, and took the knife to slay him. But an angel of the Lord called from heaven: "Abraham! lay not thy hand upon the lad, neither do thou any thing unto him: for now I know that thou fearest God, seeing thou hast not withheld thy son, thine only son, from me. By myself have I sworn, saith the Eternal, for because thou hast done this thing: that in blessing I will bless thee, and thy posterity shall be multiplied as the stars of the heaven, and as the sand upon the sea-shore; and thy posterity shall possess the gate of their enemies: *and through thy posterity shall all the nations of the earth be blessed,* because thou hast obeyed my voice." Full of joy, Abraham returned with Isaac to *Beersheba,* and dwelt there. Afterwards he moved to Hebron, where Sarah died in her one hundred and twenty-seventh year. He wept and mourned for her, and then buried her near the city of *Hebron,* in the cave of *Mach-*

pelah, which he had bought from the Hethites for four
hundred pieces (Shekel) of silver, to make it the burying-
place for his family. This cave can be seen even to this day.

---

§ 13.   ABRAHAM'S PATERNAL SOLICITUDE FOR HIS SON
ISAAC. [Genesis xxiv.-xxvi.]

When Abraham had grown old and well stricken in
age, he sent his faithful servant *Eliezer* to *Haran,* to
choose from his relatives who lived there, a wife for his
son Isaac. Eliezer took ten camels, loaded them with
various goods, started upon his journey, and arrived at
Haran towards evening. It was just the time when the
women came out to draw water from the well where he
stopped. Eliezer, who knew that no undertaking could
succeed without the help of God, offered up his prayer,
saying: "Lord, God of Abraham! I pray Thee, let me
find favor before Thee this day. Behold! I stand here by
the well of water; and the daughters of the men of the
city come out to draw water. And let it come to pass,
that the damsel to whom I shall say, Let down thy pitcher,
I pray thee, that I may drink; and shall say, Drink, and
I will give thy camels drink also, let it be a token unto
me that thou, O God! hast appointed her for Thy servant
Isaac, and thereby showest mercy unto my master." No
sooner had Eliezer ended his prayer, than REBEKAH, the
daughter of *Bethuel,* and granddaughter of *Nahor,*
Abraham's brother, came with her pitcher upon her
shoulder to draw water. Eliezer ran to meet her, and
said: "Let me, I pray thee, drink a little water of thy
pitcher." And she answered: "Drink, my lord, and I
will give thy camels drink also." Eliezer wondered at the
generosity and obliging manners of the maiden, gave her
precious rings, and asked her whose daughter she was,
and whether there was no room in her father's house for
him to lodge in that night. Rebekah said: "I am the
daughter of Bethuel and granddaughter of Nahor; we
have both straw and provender enough for thy camels, and
room for thee to lodge in for the night." Eliezer thanked

God that He had shown him the right way to the house of his master. In the meanwhile, Rebekah ran home, and there related all that had happened. When *Laban*, the brother of Rebekah, saw the beautiful gifts which his sister had received, he hastened to meet Eliezer, and said to him: "Come in, thou blessed of the Lord." Eliezer went with him to his home, where viands were placed before him. But he would not sit down to eat, until he had ascertained that Rebekah could go with him. She, as well as her parents and brother, consented to the proposal of marriage; and on the following morning, Rebekah and her maidens mounted the camels to follow Eliezer to Canaan, where she became the wife of Isaac.

At that time, Abraham was 140 years old. He lived to a quiet old age of 175 years, when he died, and was buried by his sons Isaac and Ishmael, in the cave of Machpelah, by the side of his wife Sarah.

---

§ 14. Isaac.

Isaac was, like his father Abraham, a God-fearing, kind-hearted, just, and peaceful man. He lived in Canaan, but afterwards, a famine visiting the land, he removed to *Gerar*, a city belonging to the land of the *Philistines.* Here God repeated to him the promise given to Abraham, that *"in his posterity all the nations of the earth should be blessed,"* and crowned all his undertakings with success; his herds multiplied greatly, and he had many man-servants and maid-servants. He learned also agriculture, with which his father had not been acquainted, sowed all kinds of grain, and made an exceedingly rich harvest. But his wealth roused the envy of his neighbors, who caused him many and bitter annoyances. They stopped all the wells which Abraham had digged, and Abimelech, the king of the Philistines, at last said to him: "Go from us; for thou art much mightier than we." Isaac departed thence, and pitched his tent in the valley of Gerar, and dwelt there. But as soon as he had there also opened the wells

of water which his father had digged, the herdsmen of
Gerar began to strive with his herdsmen, saying: "The
water is ours." Isaac yielded, and digged another well:
but they forced him again to give it up. He then digged
a third well, for which they would no longer contend.

When Isaac, some time after, moved to Beersheba,
Abimelech, with several of his high officers, went to see
him. And Isaac said to them: "Wherefore come ye to
me, seeing ye hate me, and have sent me away from you?"
Hereupon they answered: "We saw certainly that the
Eternal was with thee; therefore, we desire to make a
covenant with thee, that thou wilt do us no hurt, as we have
not touched thee, and as we have done unto thee nothing
but good, and have sent thee away in peace." Then Isaac
made them a feast, and they did eat and drink. And they
rose up betimes in the morning, and swore one another
concerning their covenant, and Isaac accompanied them
upon their departure, and they departed from him in
peace.

---

§ 15. Jacob and Esau. [Genesis xxv. xxvi.]

Isaac and Rebekah had been married twenty years,
when God gave them twin sons, whom they called Esau and
Jacob. Esau, the elder-born, was of a wild and rough
disposition, but Jacob was of a quiet and mild temper.
Esau who delighted in hunting, was the favorite of Isaac,
while Rebekah loved Jacob more than her elder son, because the former preferred the quiet seclusion of home to
the wild sports of the field. These brothers did not continue for a long time to live in peace with each other.
One day when Esau returned home from hunting, very
much fatigued, he found Jacob with a mess of pottage just
prepared by him, and, longing for it, he requested his
brother to give it to him. But Jacob said: "First sell
me thy birthright." Esau answered: "Behold! I am at
the point to die, and what profit can this birthright do to
me?" Hereupon he sold it to Jacob, did eat and drink,
and went away. And thus he *despised* the privileges of
his birthright.

Isaac, who did not know any thing of this transaction, at another time said to Esau: "Behold I am old, and the day of my death cannot be far distant. Now, therefore, take, I pray thee, thy weapons, thy quiver and thy bow, and go out to the field and get me some venison. And prepare it well for me, in a manner as I love it, and bring it to me, that I may eat, and then I will bless thee before I die." Rebekah, who heard this, and wished that *Jacob* should receive the last and very important blessing of his father, prepared a kid of the goat's, and persuaded Jacob to carry it in to his father, and present himself as his brother Esau. After some hesitation, Jacob yielded. Isaac, who did not recognize him, as he was almost blind, pronounced his blessing over him. But no sooner had Jacob left his father, than Esau entered with the venison and asked for his fathers's benediction. Now the deception was discovered. Esau wept for anger, and exclaimed: "The supplanter hath deceived me these two times; he took away my birthright, and now he has taken away my father's blessing!" From that time Esau entertained deep hatred against his brother, and even resolved to kill him after the death of their father. Rebekah heard of Esau's intention, and said therefore to Jacob: "Flee to Laban, my brother, to *Haran,* and stay with him until thy brother's anger turn away. Why should I be deprived of you both in one day?" She prevailed also upon Isaac to let him go, who sent him away with his blessing and with the admonition not to take a wife from the Canaanites around them, but go to the birth-place and family of his mother Rebekah. Thus Jacob fled from his home and started upon his journey to his uncle *Laban,* who lived in *Haran.*

---

§ 16. JACOB'S JOURNEY TO HARAN. [Gen. xxviii. xxix.]

Jacob left Beer-sheba and went toward Haran. On his way he was overtaken by the night, before he had reached an inhabited place. He took a stone for a pillow under his head, and fell asleep. While he was asleep, he had a

beautiful dream.   He beheld a ladder set up on the earth,
and the top of it reached to heaven, and the angels of God
ascending and descending on it.   And God stood above it,
and said: "I am the Eternal, the God of Abraham and the
God of Isaac; the land whereon thou liest, to thee will I
give it, and to thy posterity.   I will multiply thee to be
as numerous as the dust of the earth, and thou shalt spread
abroad to the west, and to the east, and to the north, and
to the south, *and through thee and through thy posterity
shall all the families of the earth be blessed.*   Behold! I
am with thee, and will keep thee in all places whither thou
goest, and will bring thee again into this land; and I
will not leave thee until I have done that of which I have
spoken to thee."   When Jacob awoke from his sleep, he
said: "Surely the Eternal is in this place; and I knew it
not.   How awful is this place; it is nothing but the house
of God, and this is the gate of heaven."   He rose early
in the morning, took the stone which had served him
for a pillow, set it up for a pillar of memorial, poured oil
upon it, and called the name of the place *Bethel*, which
signifies the *House of God.*   He made, at the same time,
a vow, saying: "If God will be with me, and will keep
me in the way that I go, and will give me bread to eat
and raiment to put on, and I come again to my father's
house in peace, then this pillar of memorial shall become
a house of God, and of all that Thou shalt give me I will
surely give the tenth unto Thee."   Hereupon Jacob continued his way towards the east, and came to a well in
the field, by which he found three flocks of sheep lying.
He asked the herdsmen: "My brethren, whence are ye?"
And they answered: "of Haran are we."   And he continued, asking: "Do you know Laban, the grandson of
Nahor?"   To which they answered: "We know him
well; and behold, Rachel his daughter, cometh with the
sheep."   When Jacob saw Rachel, he rolled the stone
from the well's mouth, and watered her flock, and wept
aloud for joy.   He told her, at the same time, that he
was the son of Rebekah, the sister of her father.   Rachel
ran home and told her father.   Laban immediately came
to the well, embraced and kissed Jacob, brought him to
his house, and made him overseer of his flocks.

§ 17. Jacob's Sojourn with Laban. [Genesis xxix. xxx.]

After the expiration of a month, Laban said to Jacob; "Wilt thou serve me for nothing; tell me, what shall thy wages be?" Jacob answered: "I will serve thee seven years if thou wilt give me thy younger daughter *Rachel* for my wife." Laban consented; and Jacob served seven years for Rachel; but they seemed to him only a few days for the ardent love which he entertained for her. But Laban deceived him, and gave him his elder daughter *Leah*, instead of Rachel to be his wife. Jacob called him to account for his deception, and said: "Why hast thou done this unto me? Did I not serve thee for Rachel? Wherefore then hast thou beguiled me giving me Leah instead of Rachel?" Laban answered: "It is not the custom in our country to give the younger before the first-born. Serve me seven more years and then I will give thee also Rachel for thy wife." Jacob did so, and Laban gave him Rachel his daughter to his wife. Jacob had the following twelve sons with Leah, Rachel, Zilpah, and Billah: *Reuben, Simeon, Levi, Judah, Dan, Naphtali, Gad, Asher, Issachar, Zebulun, Joseph,* and *Benjamin.* He had but one daughter, called *Dinah.*

After the birth of his eleventh son, Joseph, Jacob desired to return to his own country, but was induced by Laban to stay longer. Thus he served Laban most faithfully, fourteen years for his wives and six more years for wages, working hard, both by day and by night, for his avaricious father-in-law, who often attempted to defraud him of his wages. But God blessed him the more abundantly, so that he had a multitude of servants, cattle, camels and asses.

When Laban saw that Jacob's wealth increased, he showed him no longer the same friendly countenance as before, while his sons, on their part, would use slanderous language against him. It was then that God said to Jacob: "Return unto the land of thy fathers, and I will be with thee." Jacob sent and called Rachel and Leah to him into the field, and said to them: I see that your father's countenance is no more towards me as before.

But you know that with all my power I have served your
father. And he has deceived me, and changed my wages
ten times; but God suffered him not to hurt me. And
now the Eternal has said to me: 'Arise, get thee out from
this land, and return unto the land of thy kindred.' Are
ye also willing to follow God's admonition?" And Leah
and Rachel answered: "Whatever God has said unto thee
do." One day, when Laban had gone to shear his sheep
Jacob secretly departed with his wives, children, and
goods, to return to his father Isaac, to Canaan.

§ 18. Jacob's Return to his Native Country.
[Genesis xxxi.]

Three days had already elapsed since the departure of
Jacob from the house of Laban, when the latter heard of
it, hastened to pursue him, and overtook him in the mount
of *Gilead*. But God said to Laban in a dream by night:
"Take heed that thou speak unto Jacob nothing but
friendly words." Laban proposed a reconciliation with
Jacob; they ate and drank together. made a covenant,
and then separated. Jacob then continued his journey in
peace. But the nearer he approached his native country,
the stronger grew his fears of Esau, his brother. He
therefore sent messengers to him, saying: I have sojourned with Laban, and stayed there until now; and I
have oxen, and asses, flocks, and men-servants, and women-
servants, and I have sent to tell thee, that I may find grace
in thy sight." The messengers returned to Jacob, saying: "We came to thy brother Esau, and also he cometh
to meet thee, and four hundred men with him." When
Jacob heard this, he became greatly alarmed; but his
alarm did not check his activity and carefulness. With
great precaution he arranged the people that were with
him, and his flocks, in a manner that would at least secure
the safety of a part of them, in case of an attack by his
brother. He then sent presents to his brother to appease
his anger, and prayed to God for help, saying: "O God
of my fathers, the Lord who said unto me, 'Return unto

thy country and to thy kindred, and I will deal well with thee:' I am not worthy of the least of all the mercies and of all the truth which thou hast showed unto Thy servant; for I had nothing but this my staff when I passed over this Jordan, and now I return with two camps. Deliver me, I pray Thee, from the hand of my brother, from the hand of Esau: for I fear him, lest he will come and smite me, and the mother with the children." He then sent the presents, and remained that night near the brook *Jabbok*. Early in the morning, when the sun arose, he saw Esau with his four hundred men approach. But Esau, who had perceived and appreciated the exertions of Jacob for reconciliation, no sooner beheld his brother and his numerous company, than he was suddenly changed, banished all anger from his heart, ran to meet him, and embraced him, and fell on his neck and kissed him, and they wept for joy. Esau would not accept the proffered gifts, and yielded only to the urgent entreaties of Jacob. The latter then proceeded to Succoth, where he remained for a time, and then removed to *Shalem* in the land of Canaan. Here he said to his household, and to all who were with him: "Purify yourselves, and change your garments; and let us arise and go up to Beth-el, and I will build there an altar unto God, who answered me on the day of my distress, and was with me in the way which I went." And they went to Beth-el, were Jacob fulfilled his vow which he had made there on his flight from his brother Esau. During their stay in this place, *Deborah*, Rebekah's nurse, died, and her loss was greatly bewailed.

In Beth-el, God appeared to Jacob and gave him the name of ISRAEL, which signifies *Champion of God*, and promised him also that his posterity should inherit the land of Canaan. From this name *Israel*, we derive that of ISRAELITES. From Beth-el Jacob moved to *Bethlehem*. On the way, when already near the city, his beloved Rachel died, and Jacob buried her by the roadside, and set up a monument upon her grave, which is shown even to this day. From Bethlehem Jacob went to *Hebron* to his father, who died at the age of one hundred and eighty years, after having experienced the joy of seeing once more his younger son. Esau and Jacob buried him in the family sepulchre of Abraham.

The two brothers did not dwell together for a long time. Their riches were too large to allow them to stay in the same place together. Esau went with his family to mount *Seir*, and became the progenitor of the *Edomites*.

---

§ 19. The Brothers of Joseph Selling him through Envy.
[Genesis xxxviii.]

Of all his sons, Jacob loved Joseph, the elder-born son of his beloved Rachel, the most: for he was an affectionate, handsome, and intelligent lad. But his brothers envied and hated him on account of the partial fondness with which their father clung to him. And their hatred grew still stronger, when he once related to them, with innocent joy, two of his dreams, which seemed to intimate that he should at some future time rule over them. "I have dreamed," he said to them, "that we were binding sheaves in the field, and lo! my sheaf arose, and also stood upright; but your sheaves stood round about, and made obeisance to my sheaf." At another time he told them the following dream, saying, "The sun and the moon and eleven stars made obeisance to me;" meaning thereby that his father, his mother, and his eleven brothers bowed down to him. Besides, he proved to be a talebearer, telling his father whatever evil his brothers did. All these things together roused their hatred so greatly that they could not even bear his sight.

One day, the brothers of Joseph having gone to a distant pasture-ground with their flocks, Jacob said to him: "Go, I pray thee, and see whether it be well with thy brethren, and well with the flocks; and bring me word again." Joseph at once obeyed the bidding of his father and departed. But he returned no more. When his brothers saw him afar off, they said to each other: "Behold, the dreamer cometh; come now, and let us slay him, and cast him into some pit, and we will say, some evil beast has devoured him: and we shall see what will become of his dreams." But Reuben said: "Why will you slay him? Shed no blood, but cast him rather into one of the pits, and lay no hand upon him." It was the intention of Reuben secretly to take him again out of the pit and to deliver him to his father. When Joseph was come unto his brothers, they stript him of his coat of many colors, and cast him into one of the empty pits. Now it happened that, while Reuben was absent, Ishmaelitish merchants passed by, being on their way to Egypt (called *Mizraim*) with spicery, balm, and myrrh. And Judah said to his brothers: "What profit is it if we slay our brother, and conceal his blood? Come, and let us sell him to the Ishmaelites, and let not our hand be upon him; for he is our brother and our flesh.' This proposition was adopted; and Joseph was sold for twenty pieces of silver, and carried away by the Ishmaelites without mercy. When Reuben returned to the pit and found Joseph no more, he rent his clothes, and exclaimed: "The child is no more; and I, whither shall I go?" But the brother's took Joseph's coat, killed a kid of the goats, dipped the coat in the blood, sent it in this state to their father, and said: This coat we have found; know now whether it be thy son's coat or not? To his great terror, Jacob recognized the coat of his favorite child. Full of agony he rent his clothes, and filled his tent with the heart-rending cry: "Alas! alas! it is my son's coat; an evil beast has devoured him; Joseph is rent in pieces."

All his sons and daughters came to comfort him; but he refused to be comforted, saying: "No, I will go down into the dark grave unto my son mourning." Thus did his father weep for, and mourn over Joseph.

§ 20. JOSEPH A SLAVE. [Genesis xxxix.]

God turned the evil designs of Jacob's sons unto good. The Ishmaelites sold Joseph to *Potiphar*, the captain of the body-guard of the king of Egypt. Joseph, however, was not disheartened, but piously bore his unfortunate condition. He served his master faithfully and honestly, and God made all that he did prosper in his hand. For this reason his master loved him greatly, and confided his whole household to his care. But he can not yet be called altogether strong, who knows only how to bear *outward* adversity. Joseph was destined to attain greatness; therefore, he had to undergo trials, whether he could withstand also *inward* temptations and strifes. Soon an opportunity presented itself for such trials. Potiphar had a very wicked and corrupt wife, who made every exertion to mislead Joseph to faithlessness. But he remained faithful to his God and to piety, exclaiming: "How can I do this great evil and sin against my God?" As often as she urged upon him to do evil, he fled from her. She became angry and resolved to take revenge. She accused him, before Potiphar, of the very evil deed to which she had made frequent attempts to mislead him. Potiphar believed his treacherous wife, and ordered that he should be thrown into the prison where the kings' prisoners were confined. His order was immediately carried into execution.

21. Joseph in Prison. [Genesis xl.]

Joseph was now in prison. But here also he did not lose his fortitude and courage, and God was with him. By his good behaviour he won the favor of the keeper of the prison, who allowed him many privileges, and made him overseer over all his fellow-prisoners. Among these there were also two officers of the king, the chief butler and the chief baker of the royal court. Both had, in one night, very remarkable dreams which alarmed them greatly. When Joseph observed their sadness, he asked them, saying: "Wherefore look ye so sadly to-day?" They answered: "We have dreamed a dream, and can find no one to interpret it." And Joseph said unto them: "*Interpretations belong unto God alone;* yet tell me your dreams, I pray you." And the chief butler told his dream, saying: "In my dream, behold, a vine was before me; and in the vine were three branches; and it was as though it budded, and the blossoms shot forth; and the clusters thereof brought forth ripe grapes. And I took the grapes and pressed them into Pharaoh's cup, and I gave the cup into Pharaoh's hand." Joseph said to him: "The three branches signify three days. Within three days shall Pharaoh restore thee unto thy place. And then think also on me, when it shall be well with thee, and show kindness, I pray thee, unto me, and pray unto the king, that he may deliver me from this prison. For, indeed, I have done nothing that I should have deserved to be put into the dungeon." This interpretation pleased the chief baker, and he then told his dream to Joseph, saying: "I had three baskets on my head, and in the uppermost basket there was all manner of bake-meats for Pharaoh; and the birds did eat them out of the basket upon my head." And Joseph answered and said: "The three baskets signify three days. Within three days shall Pharaoh lift up thy head from off thee, and shall hang thee on a tree, and the birds shall eat thy flesh from off thee." These interpretations were fulfilled; but the chief butler forgot Joseph, and remembered him no more in his prosperity.

----

§ 22. The Release of Joseph. [Genesis xli.]

Two years afterwards, the king himself dreamed that he stood by the river, and he saw seven fat-fleshed kine, and after them seven lean-fleshed ones come up out of the river. And the latter ate up the former, and yet it could not be known that they had eaten them. After this dream Pharaoh awoke, but fell again asleep and had another ·dream. He saw seven rank and good ears of corn grow up from the earth, and after them seven others that were thin and parched; and the latter devoured the former. Of all the wise men of Egypt, whom the king consulted in the morning, not one could interpret these strange dreams. And now the chief butler remembered Joseph, and spoke to Pharaoh of his skill in the interpretation of dreams. Joseph was immediately taken from the prison, and handsomely dressed, brought before Pharaoh, who said to him: "I have heard that thou understandest well to interpret dreams." To which Joseph modestly answered: "Not *I* but *God* shall give Pharaoh an answer of peace. But relate, I pray thee, thy dreams unto me." The king then told him his dreams; and God gave Joseph the wisdom to tnterpret them. He, consequently, addressed the king, saying: "What God is about to do, He showeth unto Pharaoh. Behold, there will come seven years of great plenty throughout all the land of Egypt. And there shall arise after them seven years of famine. Now, therefore, let Pharaoh erect storehouses, and gather, during the seven plenteous years, the fifth part of all the corn of Egypt, and lay it up for store to the land against the seven years of famine; that the land perish not through the famine." Pharaoh, greatly pleased with his speech, said to Joseph: "Forasmuch as God has granted thee so much wisdom and understanding, thou shalt be over my house, and I shall set thee over all the land of Egypt." Thereupon he took off his ring from his hand, and put it upon Joseph's hand, (as a token that the latter could henceforth decree laws in the name of the king,) and arrayed him in garments of fine linen, and put a gold chain about his neck, and caused the following proclamation to be made: "Bow the knee: this is your ruler!" Pharaoh gave him also the daughter of an Egyptian high-priest to wife.

The poor prisoner slave thus all at once became chief minister of a king of Egypt. Joseph then travelled all over the land of Egypt, gathered corn during the years of plenty, and laid it up in storehouses with the most prudent care for the years of famine. And as he had predicted, the years of dearth came, and famine, distress, and misery reigned in all neighboring countries, while the Egyptians were still provided with bread. But when their provisions were exhausted, they cried to Pharaoh for bread. And Pharaoh said to them: "Go unto Joseph; what he saith to you, do." Joseph then opened the storehouses and provided the Egyptians with corn. And the people of other countries also came to Joseph to buy corn from him.

---

§ 23. THE FIRST JOURNEY OF JOSEPH'S BROTHERS TO EGYPT. [Genesis xlii.]

The land of Canaan suffered likewise by this famine. And Jacob said to his sons: "I have heard that there is corn in Egypt: get you down thither and buy for us from thence, that we may live and not die." The sons of Jacob departed upon their journey; but Benjamin, Joseph's brother, Jacob did not send with them, fearing lest some evil accident might befall him. They arrived safely in Egypt, appeared before Joseph, bowed down themselves before him with their faces to the earth, but did not recog nize him, both on account of the brilliant attire of his royal grandeur, and because the lad whom they had sold, when seventeen years old, was then a man of thirty-eight years. Joseph, on the other hand, at once recognized them, and remembered the dreams he had had in the days of his youth. Although it was now in his power to punish them for their cruel conduct towards him, he banished every thought of revenge from his bosom; he still loved his brothers, and had long forgiven them. Intending, however, to try them, and see whether they had become better men, he made them believe that he did not know them, and asked them with feigned harshness: "Whence do you come?" They answered with trembling voices: "We are come from Canaan, to buy food." "No," replied Joseph, "I know ye better; ye are spies; to see the nakedness of the land ye are come." Submissively they answered: "Pardon Lord! we are come to buy food. We are honest men; thy servants are no spies. We are twelve brethren, the sons of *one* man, the youngest alone is with our father, and the other—is no more." Joseph would no longer listen to them, but said: "It is so, as I have said to you, ye are spies." He then sent them into prison, but already on the third day he had them again brought before him, and said to them: "I fear God, and would do injustice to no man. If ye be true men, let one of your brethren be bound in the house of your prison; go ye, carry corn for the famine of your houses. But bring your youngest brother unto me, so shall your words be verified, and ye shall not die." Now their grief increased. Conscience-stricken they spoke to each other, in Hebrew: "We are indeed guilty concerning our brethren, in that we saw the anguish of his soul when he besought us, and we would not hear; therefore is this distress come upon us." And Reuben answered them, saying: "Spake I not unto you, saying, Do not sin against the child, and ye would not hear? therefore, behold, also his blood is required." They did not know that Joseph understood their language. When he heard their words, he could not suppress his tears; he turned away and wept. He now perceived that they had become better. However, as he desired to increase their feelings of repentance, he ordered that Simeon, who had no doubt shown himself to be the most unfeeling of them, should be bound before them, and sent him into prison. He then commanded to fill the sacks of his other brothers with corn, to restore, unknown to them, every man's money into his sack, and dismissed them. They laded their asses with the corn and departed. On their way one of them opened his sack to give his ass provender, and found to his great astonishment, his money therein. All were filled with dread, saying one to another: "Why hath God done this unto us?" Arrived at home they emptied their sacks, and, behold! every one found his bundle of money in his sack. They then told their father all that had happened during their journey and their stay in Egypt. When Jacob had heard their narrative, he cried, and said: "Ye will yet bereave me of all my children: Joseph is no more, Simeon is no more, and now ye will take also Benjamin away. All these things are against me!" And Reuben answered his father, saying: "Deliver him into my hand; I will bring him to thee again. I will leave my two sons as hostages, that I shall fulfill my promise." But Jacob replied: "My son shall not go down with you; for his brother is dead, and he is left alone of the sons of his mother. If mischief befall him by the way in which ye go, then shall ye bring down my gray hairs with sorrow to the grave."

---

§ 24. The Second Journey of Joseph's Brothers to Egypt. [Genesis xliii.]

When the corn brought from Egypt was eaten up, Jacob said to his sons: "Go again, buy a little food." And Judah replied, saying: "If thou wilt send our brother

Benjamin with us, we will go to buy corn ; but without Benjamin we cannot appear before the man. Send the lad with me. I will be surety for him ; of my hand shalt thou require him : if I bring him not unto thee again, and set him before thee, then let me bear the blame forever." Jacob persisted for a long time in his refusal to send Benjamin with them. But the famine becoming greater every day, he at last consented, saying: " If it must be so now, do this: take off the best fruit of the land in your vessels, and carry down the man a present, a little balm and a little honey, spices, and myrrh, nuts, and almonds. And take double money in your hand, and the money that was brought again in your sacks, carry it again with you; peradventure it was an oversight. Take also your brother, and arise, go again unto the man. And God Almighty may give you mercy before the man, that he may send away your other brother and Benjamin. But if I be bereaved of my children, be it so !" The sons of Jacob then departed to Egypt with Benjamin. When Joseph saw them, he said to the ruler of his house: " Bring these men home, and prepare a repast for them; for they shall dine with me to-day." But his brothers were afraid, when they were brought into Joseph's house, and they said: "Because of the money that was returned in our sacks at the first time are we brought in ; that he may seek occasion against us, and fall upon us, and take us for bondmen." They therefore addressed the steward of Joseph's house, and told him that they had found the money in their sacks and brought it back again. The steward answered them, saying: "Peace be with you! Fear not! Your God and the God of your father hath given you treasure in your sacks; I had your money." He then released Simeon from the prison, and brought him to them, and gave them water to wash their feet, and provender for their asses. When Joseph came home, they offered him the present which they held in their hands, and bowed themselves to him to the earth. But he greeted them very kindly and said at once to them: " Is your father well, the old man, of whom you spake? Is he yet alive?" Hereupon he looked for Benjamin, and, recognizing him, said : "Is this your younger brother of whom you spoke to me? God be gracious unto thee, my son!" While he spoke these words, his feelings overpowered him, he hastened away into his chamber and wept; for his heart was filled with love and tender affection. Most willingly would he have now made himself known, for he saw that they had improved. They had returned to Egypt to release their brother Simeon; they had brought back the money found in their sacks; their speeches proved that they feared God: but one thing more was wanted: Joseph not doubting that his brother Benjamin was now, as he himself in former days, the favorite of his father, was desirous to learn, whether Benjamin was in the same manner hated by them, as he himself had once been the subject of their hatred. He, therefore, commanded the steward of his house after dinner, saying: "Fill the men's sacks with food, as much as they can carry, and put every man's money in his sack's mouth. And put my cup, the silver cup, in the sack of the youngest." The steward did as Joseph had commanded. But no sooner were they gone out of the city, than the steward followed after them, at the command of Joseph, overtook them, and said to them: "Wherefore have ye rewarded evil for good? Why have ye stolen the cup of my lord?" They answered: "Wherefore saith my lord these words? God forbid that thy servants should do according to this thing. Behold, the money which we found in our sacks we brought again unto thee out of the land of Canaan: how then should we steal out of thy lord's house silver or gold? Search our sacks, and with whomsoever of thy servants the cup be found, both let him die, and we also be my lord's bondmen." Then they speedily took down every man his sack to the ground, and opened every man his sack, but, to their great horror, the cup was found in the sack of Benjamin. Horror-stricken, they rent their clothes, re-laded their asses, and returned into the city. Oh! what deep feelings of grief and alarm must have filled their hearts on their return to the house of Joseph!

§ 25. THE RECOGNITION. [Genesis xliv. xlv.]

The sons of Jacob were brought before Joseph, who addressed them saying: "What shameful deed have ye committed?" And Judah said: "What shall we say unto my lord? how can we clear ourselves? God hath found out the iniquity of thy servants, therefore this has happened unto us. Behold! we will all now be thy bondmen." But Joseph said: "God forbid that I should do so; but the man in whose hand the cup was found, he shall be my servant; as for you, get you up in peace unto your father."

Judah, remembering the promise which he had made to his father concerning Benjamin, then drew near, and spoke to Joseph with a touching voice, saying: "O my lord! let thy servant, I pray thee, speak a word in my lord's ears, and let not thine anger burn against thy servant. I have become surety for this lad, who is alone left of the sons of his mother, and our father's heart clings most lovingly to him. Thy servant our father said to us, You know that my wife bare me two sons. And the one went out from me, and I saw him not since. And if ye take this also from me, and mischief befall him, ye shall bring down my gray hairs with sorrow to the grave. Now therefore when I come to thy servant my father, and the lad be not with us, seeing that his life is bound up in the lad's life: it shall come to pass, when he seeth that the lad is not with us, that he will die, and thy servants shall bring down the gray hairs of thy servant our father with sorrow to the grave. Now, therefore, I pray thee, let me abide instead of the lad as bondman to my lord; and let the lad go home with his brothers. For how shall I go home to my father without the lad? How could I see the grief that shall come upon my father?" Joseph could no longer restrain himself—he could no longer master his feelings, and exclaimed: "Let every Egyptian go out!" When he was alone with his brothers, he wept aloud, so that he could be heard even outside of the house, and said to his brothers: "I am Joseph, doth my father yet live?" His brothers were unable to reply; for terror, shame, and joy perplexed their hearts and minds. Joseph kindly anticipated them, and said: "Come near to me, I pray you. I am your brother Joseph, whom you sold into Egypt. But think not that I am angry on this account. Not you, but God did send me hither, and hath made me a father unto Egypt, to preserve your lives in these years of famine. Hasten to my father, and tell him of all my glory in Egypt, and of all that you have seen. Hasten now, and bring down my father hither." After these words, he fell upon his brother Benjamin's neck and wept. And Benjamin wept upon his neck. He then kissed all his brothers and wept in their arms; and after that only, his brothers talked with him.

When Pharaoh heard that Joseph's brothers had come, he was exceedingly pleased, and commanded Joseph to give his brothers wagons and food for their journey, and besides, a festival garment to each of them: but Benjamin received five garments and three hundred pieces of silver. And to his father he sent ten asses laden with good things of Egypt, and ten she-asses laden with corn, bread and meat for his journey.

Then Joseph took leave of his brothers, and said to them on their departure: "Be not agitated by the way! All be forgotten!"

---

§ 26. The Family of Jacob Removing to Egypt.
[Genesis xlvi.].

Jacob passed the days during which all his sons were away from him, in great sadness. But his sadness was soon changed into joy. They all returned and brought him, as the best token of their welcome greeting, the intelligence that Joseph was still alive, and ruler over all the land of Egypt. The intense joy of Jacob at this intelligence may be felt, but cannot be described in words. His heart fainted, for he could hardly believe them. But when they told him all the words of Joseph, and he beheld the wagons which Joseph had sent to carry him and his family to Egypt, his spirit revived in joy, and he exclaimed: "It is enough; Joseph my son is yet alive. I will go and see him before I die. Although he was old and infirm, he nevertheless hastened to leave Canaan, and departed with his own family, consisting of seventy persons, for the land of Egypt. At the boundary of Canaan he offered sacrifices to his God.

Joseph could not wait for the arrival of his father in Egypt, he was too anxious to see him again; he mounted his chariot to meet him on the way. As soon as he saw him, he left his chariot, fell on his neck, and wept for some time in his arms. And Jacob also wept, and said; "Now let me die, because I have seen thy face, that thou art yet alive." When the family of Jacob had entered the city, Joseph presented his father and some of his brothers before Pharaoh, who asked the venerable Patriarch: "How old art thou?" Jacob replied: "The days of the years of my pilgrimage are one hundred and thirty years; few and evil have been the days of the years of my life, and have not attained unto the days of the years of the life of my fathers in the days of their pilgrimage." He then blessed Pharaoh and withdrew.

Joseph did all that lay in his power to render the remainder of Jacob's life happy and joyful. He gave him the best part of the land, the region of *Goshen*, for his dwelling place. Seventeen years afterwards, Jacob became sick. When Joseph heard it, he went with his sons *Manasseh* and *Ephraim* to see his father. Jacob said to him: "Do not bury me in the land of Egypt, but with my fathers in the cave of Machpelah, which is before Mamre, in the land of Canaan, in our family sepulchre." He then blessed the sons of Joseph, and adopted them as his own children. He then also blessed his own sons and, when finished, "he gathered up his feet into his bed, and expired." Joseph fell upon his face, and wept upon him, and kissed him. The Egyptians mourned for Jacob seventy days, after which Joseph, accompanied by his brethren and a large number of Egyptians, went to Canaan to fulfil the last wish of his father, and buried him in the cave of Machpelah.

After their return to Egypt, the brothers of Joseph feared that he, as their father was dead, might now take revenge upon them for all the evil which they had done to him, sent a messenger to him, and went afterwards

4

themselves, to implore his forgiveness for their great wrong doing. But Joseph said to them: "Fear not; I also stand under God. *Though ye thought evil against me, God meant it unto good.* Fear not, I will nourish you, and your little ones." And he faithfully performed all he had promised.

Joseph lived to such a happy old age, as to see the children and children's children of his sons *Manasseh* and *Ephraim*, and died in the one hundred and tenth year of his life, after having requested his brothers to carry his bones with them to the land of Canaan, whenever they should return thither   His body was embalmed and kept in a coffin in Egypt

III.

THE ISRAELITES IN EGYPT.

§ 27. BIRTH OF MOSES. [Exodus i. ii.]

After the death of Jacob and Joseph, the Israelites had no longer a common chieftain, but every tribe had a distinct name, taken from that of their several chieftains, that is to say, from the names of the sons of Jacob. Yet all the tribes lived in entire seclusion from the Egyptians, so that their pure knowledge of God could not be disturbed by Egyptian idolatry.

In the course of time, a new king arose, who knew not Joseph, nor the meritorious services which he had rendered Egypt, and regarded with indignation and animosity the flourishing condition and mighty increase of the Israelites. He feared their vast multitude, and apprehended that they, looked upon as they were as foreigners, might rebel, or leave the land against his will, and join his enemies. He, therefore, afflicted them with intolerable burthens, forced them to perform the most rigorous services, and treated them in the most cruel manner. And when he saw that he did not succeed in accomplishing his object by all these means, he issued the inhuman decree, that all new-born male children should be cast into the river: hoping that thus the Israelites would gradually die out. But God had so ordained it that the descendants of Jacob should be preserved, in order that He might accomplish, through them, great and miraculous deeds. The more the Israelites were afflicted, the more they multiplied and increased.

In the year 2413, after the Creation of the World, a handsome boy was born also to *Amram* and *Jochebed*, of the tribe of Levi. They hid him in their house three

months. But they could no longer conceal him; for the
eye of envy is watchful, and treachery never sleeps.
Jochebed, therefore, wove a little ark of bulrushes, put
the child into it, placed it amidst the flags by the river's
brink, and bade her daughter *Miriam* stand afar off to
watch the child. It happened then that the daughter of
the king came down to the river to bathe. She saw the
ark, and ordered one of her maids that were with her, to
take it out of the water and bring it to her. When she
opened it, and saw a weeping child in it, she exclaimed
with emotion : "Oh! this is one of the Hebrews' children."
When Miriam observed the emotion of the king's daughter,
she ran to her and said : "Shall I go and call to thee a
nurse of the Hebrew women that she may nurse the child
for thee ?" And Pharaoh's daughter replied to her : "Yes,
go." And the maid hastened and called the child's mother,
who thus had her own child returned to her from the hand
of the princess.

When the child had grown up, the daughter of Pharaoh
took him as her own son, and called him *Moses*, that is,
" the Child rescued from the Waters."

§ 28.   Moses manifesting his Attachment to his People. [Exodus ii.]

Moses, being educated at the palace of the king, had
ample opportunity to develop his talents, and learn all the
wisdom of the Egyptians, which afterwards was of great
advantage to him. The Princess herself regarded him as
her son. No doubt, if he had desired it, he could have
attained to the highest offices and dignities of Egypt, and
he could have enjoyed, at the royal court, all the pleasures
that the world could afford. But the sight of his suffering
brethren filled him with profound grief; he disdained the
glory that the Egyptians could bestow upon him, while
the sad condition of his brethren engaged all his thoughts

and feelings. Once, seeing an Egyptian cruelly beat an Israelite, he was so deeply moved by the sight that, in taking the part of his brother, he allowed his zeal to carry him so far, that he slew the Egyptian—no doubt inadvertently, in the zeal of his interference—and then hid him in the sand. On the following day he found two Hebrews striving together, and said to him who was in the wrong: "Why smitest thou thy fellow?" Upon which the man replied: "Who made thee a ruler and judge over us? intendest thou to kill me, as thou didst kill the Egyptian?" Then Moses became afraid, and said to himself: "Surely the thing is already become known." Now, when Pharaoh heard of the event, Moses was no longer secure in Egypt. He, therefore, fled to *Midian*, and sat down fatigued by his journey, near a well.

There lived a priest in Midian, named *Jethro*, who had seven daughters. These just came out with their flocks to draw water; but other shepherds came and drove them away. Moses could not endure to see this injustice, he helped the maids, and thus enabled them to water their flocks. When they had returned to their father's house, they related all that had happened. Then said Jethro: "Where is the man? why have ye not invited him here to eat?" Moses was at once sent for, and consented to dwell with Jethro, who gave him his daughter *Zipporah* for his wife, and kept henceforth the flock of his father-in-law. He had two sons, whom he called *Gershom* and *Eliezer*.

In the meanwhile, the king of Egypt died; but the condition of the Israelities grew still more miserable. "And they sighed by reason of their bondage," and they cried for help to their Father in heaven, and *He* harkened unto their lamentations.

---

§ 29. The Appointment of Moses. (Exodus iii.)

Moses, as we have just heard, kept the flock of Jethro. For many years he had led the life of a simple and modest shepherd, and reflected, in the solitude of the desert, upon the misery of his fellow-Israelites in Egypt. During this time he had acquired, moreover, that calmness and discretion which were necessary for him as the deliverer of his people from the hand of the tyrant. The heat and rashness of his youth had abated, and thus he was well matured for the plans which God had laid out concerning the redemption of Israel.

One day he tended his flock near the foot of Mount Horeb. All at once he beheld a bush in flames, and yet, the bush was not consumed. He drew near more closely to examine the appearance, when the voice of God addressed him, saying: "Moses, draw not nigh hither: put off thy shoes from thy feet, for the place whereon thou standest is holy ground." And God said furthermore: "I am the God of Abraham, of Isaac, and of Jacob. I have seen the affliction of my people, thy brethren, and have heard their lamentations, and I am come down to deliver them. Go to Pharaoh in Egypt, and demand of him that he should let my people depart from Egypt. And I am sure that the king of Egypt will not let you go; but I will stretch out my hand, and smite Egypt with all my wonders, and after that he will let you go." Moses, believing that he was not equal to such a task, would not accept the appointment, and said: "But the people of Israel will not believe me, nor hearken unto my voice, and will say: God hath not appeared unto thee." Then said God to him: "Behold! by my help the Israelites will hearken unto thy voice." Moses still hesitated to undertake the great work, and said: "Thou knowest, O my Lord! that I am not eloquent, but that I am slow of speech, and of a slow tongue." Then God answered him, saying; "Who hath made man's mouth? or who maketh the dumb, or deaf, or the seeing, or the blind? have not I the Eternal? Now, therefore, go, and I will be with thy mouth, and teach thee what thou shalt say." Moses said: "O my Lord! send him whom thou wilt send." Then said the Eternal with great force: "Do I not know that thy brother *Aaron* is very eloquent? He will come forth to meet thee, and when he seeth thee, he will be glad in his heart. He shall be thy companion and thy spokesman before the king and the people.

Moses thereupon returned to his father-in-law, took leave from him, and then started upon his journey to Egypt. While journeying through the wilderness, he met his brother Aaron, and conversed with him concerning the great task which God had intrusted to him. They then went together to Egypt, gathered together all the elders of the children of Israel, and communicated to them the will of their God. And the people believed, bowed their heads, and worshipped.

§ 30. THE DELIVERANCE OF THE ISRAELITES FROM THE EGYPTIAN BONDAGE. [Exodus xii.]

Moses and Aaron stepped before Pharaoh, and demanded of him, by virtue of God's command, to let the Israelites go on a three day's journey to celebrate a feast in the wilderness. But the heathen king proudly replied upon this demand: "Who is the Eternal, your God, that I should obey his voice, to let Israel go? I know not your God, neither will I let Israel go. There is too great a number of idle people in the land; wherefore will ye keep them from their work? Get you unto your burdens! Ye are idle, ye are idle; therefore ye say, Let us go and celebrate a feast in the desert. But now ye shall be forced to do still harder work, in order that ye may forget all desire of celebrating feasts!" And the Israelites were indeed still more oppressed, and, full of indignation, they said to Moses and Aaron: "The Lord look upon you and judge, because ye have made our savor to be abhored in the eyes of Pharaoh, and in the eyes of his servants, to put a sword in their hand to slay us." Then Moses prayed, saying: "Lord, wherefore hast Thou so evil-entreated this people? Why is it that Thou hast sent me? For since I came to Pharaoh to speak in Thy name, he hath oppressed this people still more, and Thou hast not yet delivered them." God then renewed his promise of help and protection, and the speedy delivery of the Israelites. Moses conveyed these promises to his brethren; but they would not listen to him, for anguish of spirit and for cruel bondage.

Now Moses appeared before Pharaoh, and gave him proofs of his divine mission. But the heart of Pharaoh was hardened, and he refused to let the Israelites go. On account of this obstinacy on the part of the king, God sent ten great plagues upon Egypt. He changed all the waters of the land to blood, and brought frogs, vermin, flies, murrain, small-pox, hail, locusts, and deep darkness all over the country; but Pharaoh hardened his heart and hearkened not unto Moses. As long as each plague lasted, he promised to obey and permit the Israelites to depart; but as soon as it was removed, he retracted all his promises. Then said God: " Yet will I bring one plague more upon Pharaoh and upon Egypt; afterwards he will let you go. About midnight all the first-born in the land of Egypt shall die, from the first-born of the king, even unto the first-born of the maid-servant that is behind the mill, but not the least evil shall befall the Israelites. This one plague I shall yet bring upon Pharaoh and his land, and then he will let you go. And now prepare the last repast in Egypt! Kill every man a lamb, one lamb for a house, take of the blood and sprinkle it on the two side-posts and on the upper door-post of the houses, and eat the flesh with unleavened bread and bitter herbs; and ye shall eat it with your loins girded, your shoes on your feet, and your staff in your hand, to be perfectly ready for a journey."

The plague thus foretold by God was brought upon Egypt. In the night of the fourteenth day of the month of *Nisan,** all the first-born of Egypt died, from the first-born of the king even to the cattle. And there was a great lamentation throughout the land; for there was not even *one* house in which there was not one dead. Only the houses of the Israelites, in which the *Passover-sacrifice* was brought, escaped. Now the proud Pharaoh hastened himself to Moses and requested him to depart with all the

---

* The names of the Jewish months are as fol'ows : *Nisan. Iyar, Sivan, Tamooz, Ab, Elool, Tishri, Marheshvan, Kislev, Tebet, Shebat, Adar* and, (in a leap-year,) *Second Adar.*

people of Israel from Egypt, and take everything with them which belonged to them. And the Egyptians were likewise urgent upon the people to hasten their departure, for they said: "We shall be all dead men!" They would not even leave them sufficient time to leaven the dough prepared for bread, so that the Israelites were compelled to take it with them unleavened and unbaked, lest they were without food at the very beginning of their journey.

Thus God delivered them from their bondage. About six hundred thousand men, that could bear arms, left Egypt, and with them a great number of mixed people, beside large flocks and herds, after they had suffered under cruel bondage almost two hundred years. Notwithstanding the great haste in which the Israelites departed from Egypt, Moses did not forget to take the bones of Joseph with him. At the command of God, they journeyed towards the *Red Sea*. God also commanded the Israelites to commemorate their delivery from Egypt every year, for all times, by the celebration of the *Festival of Passover*, and to eat unleavened bread (*Mazoth*) during the seven days of this festival.

---

§ 31. The Destruction of Pharaoh. [Exodus xiv.]

The chastisements of God struck Pharaoh and the Egyptians only with transient dread, but did not effect their complete improvement. The Israelites had not yet made many day's journey from Egypt, when the king regretted their departure and started upon their pursuit, to drive them back into bondage. Not far from the Red Sea he overtook them. The Israelites were in great danger; before them was the sea, behind them the pursuing enemy, and to their right and left they saw steep rocks. Moses comforted them in their fright, saying: "Fear not, trust in the help of God, He shall fight for you; to-day you shall once more see the Egyptians, and ye shall see them no more forever." In the name of God he then stretched forth his staff over the sea, and a strong east wind began to blow, and made the sea dry land, and the waters were divided. Now the children of Israel passed through the midst of the sea upon the dry ground, and the waters were a wall unto them on their right hand and on their left. They had already reached the opposite shores, when the Egyptians hastened after them in blind pursuit. But Moses again, at the command of God, stretched forth his staff over the sea, the waves returned and buried the chariots and the horsemen, and all the host of Pharaoh that came into the sea after them ; not even one man escaped.

When the Israelites saw the Egyptians dead upon the sea-shore, the people feared the Eternal, and believed both HIM AND HIS SERVANT MOSES; then sang Moses and the children of Israel a song of thanks and praise unto the Eternal. And Miriam also, the sister of Aaron, took a timbrel in her hand, and sang with all the women : "Sing ye unto the Eternal, for He is high and exalted ; the horse and his rider hath he thrown into the sea!"

§ 32. THE PROCLAMATION OF THE LAW ON MOUNT SINAI. [Exodus xx.]

From the Red Sea the Israelites moved towards the *desert*, a desolate and uninhabited country. They intended thence to go to Canaan, where their forefathers had sojourned, and which God had promised to give them for an inheritance. In the third month after their departure from Egypt, the Israelites came to the wilderness of Mount SINAI and encamped there. Here God said unto Moses: "Thus shalt thou say to the house of Jacob, and proclaim to the children of Israel : 'Ye have seen what I did unto the Egyptians, and how I bare you as upon the protecting wings of an eagle, and brought you hither. Now, therefore, if ye will obey my commandments, ye shall be a peculiar possession unto me, though the whole earth is mine. AND YE SHALL BE UNTO ME A KINGDOM OF PRIESTS, AND A HOLY NATION.' These are the words which thou shalt speak unto the children of Israel." Moses then called the elders of the people together, and communicated these words to them. The whole people answered together, exclaiming: "All that the Eternal hath spoken we will do." Now God spoke to Moses furthermore, saying: "Tell the children of Israel that they should sanctify themselves, wash their clothes. and be prepared for the third day. And on the third day, they shall appear at the foot of the mountain." And it came to pass on the third day, that there were heavy thunders and lightnings, and a thick cloud upon the mount, and the sound of the cornet was heard, growing more and more powerful. Fear seized upon all the people; the whole mountain stood in flames, smoked, and quaked. Then all was silent again, and the voice of God spoke distinctly, as follows:

1. *I am the Eternal thy God, who hath brought thee out of the land of Egypt, from the house of bondage.*

2. *Thou shalt have no other gods before me. Thou shalt not make unto thee any graven image, or any likeness of any thing that is in heaven above, or that is on the earth beneath, or that is in the water under the earth; thou shalt not bow down before them, nor worship them; for I, the Eternal thy God, am a jealous God, visiting the guilt of the fathers upon the children unto the third and fourth generation of them that hate me; but showing mercy unto thousands of them that love me and keep my commandments.*

3. *Thou shalt not utter the name of the Eternal thy God unto falsehood; for the Eternal will not let him go unpunished who uttereth His name unto falsehood.*

4. *Remember the Sabbath-day to keep it holy. Six days shalt thou labor and do all thy work; but the seventh day is a day of rest unto the Eternal thy God. On it thou shalt do no manner of work, thou nor thy son, nor thy daughter, thy man-servant, nor thy maid-servant, nor thy cattle, nor the stranger that sojourneth within thy gates. For in six days the Eternal made heaven and earth, the sea and all that in them is, and rested on the seventh day; therefore God blessed the Sabbath-day and hallowed it.*

5. *Honor thy father and thy mother, that thy days may last long in the land which the Eternal thy God giveth thee.*

6. *Thou shalt not murder.*

7. *Thou shalt not commit adultery.*

8. *Thou shalt not steal.*

9. *Thou shalt not testify against thy neighbor as a false witness.*

10. *Thou shalt not covet thy neighbor's house, thou shalt not covet thy neighbor's wife, nor his man-servant, nor his maid-servant, nor his ox, nor his ass, nor any thing that is thy neighbor's.*

All the people heard these words and said trembling and fearing: "All that the Lord hath spoken we will do, and we will obey him." (*Origin of the* FESTIVAL OF THE WEEKS.)

---

§ 33.   THE ISRAELITES WORSHIPPING THE GOLDEN CALF.
[Genesis xxxii.]

Shortly after the proclamation of the Law, God spoke to Moses, saying: "Come up to me into the mount, and I will give thee tables of stone, and laws, and commandments, which I have written." And Moses rose up, and went up into the mount of God, entered the cloud, and tarried there, and remained there forty days and forty nights.   Impatient of the long absence of Moses, and believing that Moses must have died, the people said to Aaron: "Make us gods, for we know not what is become of that man Moses who brought us out of the land of Egypt." Aaron had not sufficient courage to resist the demands of the people, and made for them a golden calf, which they worshipped, exclaiming: "These are thy gods, O Israel! that brought thee up out of the land of Egypt!" When Moses came down from the mountain he saw with horror that the people had forsaken their God to worship an idol, and was seized with such holy indignation, that he cast down the tables of stone which he had received from God, and broke them before their feet.   He then boldly stepped amidst the apostate Israelites, took the golden calf from before their eyes, destroyed it, and commanded the tribe of Levi, that had alone remained true to the God of Israel, to punish the Idolaters. They slew about three thousand of the *calf-worshippers.* On the following morning, however, Moses said unto the people: "Ye have committed a great sin; and now I will go up unto God and invoke his forgiveness upon you." And he prayed to God: "O Lord! forgive the people! If not, blot me, I pray thee, out of Thy book." And the Lord said unto Moses: "Whoever hath sinned against me, him will I blot out of my book. Yet, I have pardoned the people according to thy word." Moses was so full of grateful veneration for the goodness of God, that he felt the ardent desire still more to know Him, and prayed: "O God! If I have found grace in Thy eyes, show me Thy ways, that I may know the." Then said God: "No man can ever have a perfect conception of my being; but know, *God is eternal, unchangeable, almighty, merciful, gracious, long-suffering, full of love and truth, preserving his mercy even for thousands, forgiving iniquity, transgression and sin, but permitting no guilt to go unpunished.*" Hereupon God gave Moses two new tables of stone and dismissed him. When Moses came down from the mountain to the people, his countenance shone with such a brilliant halo, that he had to put on a veil, because the people were afraid to approach him.

---

§ 34. RITUAL INSTITUTIONS—THE TABERNACLE OF THE COVENANT — THE PRIESTS — THE LEVITES. [Exodus xxv.-xl.]

The Eternal spoke to Moses, saying: "Speak unto the children of Israel, that they bring me an offering: of every man that giveth it willingly with his heart, ye shall take it, gold, silver, brass, purple, fine linen, skins, furs, oil, spices, and jewels, and let them make me a sanctuary after the pattern that I shall show thee, that I may dwell amongst them." Moses did as God had commanded him, and behold! far more offerings were brought than were required.

Israelites skilful in all manner of workmanship, immediately began to build the Holy Tabernacle. The whole
5

was thirty cubits long, ten cubits broad, and ten cubits high, constructed of forty eight boards of shittim wood covered with gold. These boards were held together by five gilded bars, passing through five golden rings fixed on each of the boards. Four coverings were spread over the Tabernacle, one above the other. At the entrance of the Tabernacle was a curtain of blue, and scarlet, and purple, of fine twined linen, wrought with needlework.

The *inside* of the Tabernacle consisted of two apartments. The first of these, called the *Holy Place*, was much more spacious than the second, called the *Holy of Holies*, or *Most Holy Place*. In the Holy Place stood: The *Table of Shew-Bread*, the *Golden Candlestick*, and the *Altar of Incense*.

Upon the *Table of Shew-bread*, called also the *Golden Table*, because it was overlaid with gold, lay, in two piles, the twelve loaves of unleavened bread, (shew-bread, לֶחֶם הַפָּגִים) which were changed every Sabbath

The *Golden Candlestick* had seven arms; upon the top of each was placed a lamp, filled with holy oil, and kept perpetually burning.

The *Altar of Incense* was made of shittim wood and plated with gold, one cubit in length, the same in breadth, and two cubits in height. Upon this altar sweet incense was burnt every morning and evening.

In the *Holy of Holies*, which was completely dark, stood the *Ark of the Covenant*. It was a kind of chest, made of shittim wood, and covered within and without with gold. Its lid was of purest gold, and two Cherubim, made of solid gold, was placed on the two ends, their faces turned towards each other. In this ark the two tables of stone were kept.

The Holy Tabernacle was surrounded by an outer inclosure, called *The Court of the Tabernacle*, one hundred cubits long and fifty broad, supported by columns which rested on sockets of brass, and were connected, on their tops, by means of rods, from which curtains were suspended. Within this enclosure, in the open air stood the *Altar of Burnt Offerings*, upon which the sacrificial animals were burned and sacred fire was continually kept burning. Besides this altar, the *Brazen Laver* for the use of the Priests stood in the Court of the Tabernacle.

God spoke further to Moses, saying; "Take Aaron and his sons, have holy garments made for them, and consecrate them for me to be my priests." In obedience to this command, Moses called the whole people together, brought Aaron and his sons before them, and caused Aaron to be washed. Hereupon he had him clothed with the *Coat* or *Tunic,* reaching down to his ankles; the *Upper Garment,* or the robe of the ephod, which reached down to his knees, and had upon the hem of its lower part little bells of gold and pomegranates in needlework; above it he placed the *Ephod,* the *Girdle,* and the *Breastplate* with twelve precious stones, with the names of the twelve tribes engraven upon them. He then put the *Mitre* upon his head, and on the front of it he placed the *Golden Plate,* with the inscription, *Holy unto the Eternal!* After having attired Aaron in these sacred garments, he anointed him to be the High-Priest, and his sons to be the Priests of God. The members of the tribe of Levi—the *Levites*—were appointed to be ministers in the service of the Sanctuary, and received the *Tithes* of all fruits for their sustenance; for they were excluded from the general distribution of the promised land.

Moses next communicated, according to the command of God, the laws concerning the *sacrifices* to the people. These could be offered only in the sanctuary, and through the medium of the priests. The sacrifices consisted of *wine* and *oil,* of *baked meats* and such *animals* which were declared clean and free from all bodily defect and blemish. Every morning and evening a lamb was to be offered upon the altar of the sanctuary. For the Sabbaths and Festivals especial sacrifices were instituted, as also for particular occasions: *Sin, Trespass* and *Peace Offerings.* Besides these, *Free-Will Offerings* of individuals were admitted. The manner of offering was different for the different sacrifices, and very minutely described in the law. The most solemn sacrifice was that instituted for the *Day of Atonement,* which was a day of general expiation for the whole people. On this day the High-Priest had first to offer a sin-offering for himself—for even the chief amongst the priests is not free from sin—and then another for the whole people. He then took the blood, entered the Holy of Holies—the only time throughout the year—sprinkled it upon the lid of the Ark, prayed, and blessed the Congregation.

Besides the laws concerning the sacrifices, a large number of other ritual statutes were proclaimed, and may be found in the Books of Moses.

§ 35. The Rebellions of the People, caused by their Hardships in the Wilderness.

The Israelites did not bear with patience the hardships of their wandering in the desert, but lost, on every occasion, all confidence in God, murmured, whenever they suffered from want, and then expressed the wish that they would prefer returning into their former bondage in Egypt. On all these occasions, Moses was subjected to the most harrasing and bitter reproaches. But God regarded with paternal love their want of courage and base inclinations, and provided them in the most miraculous way, with all the necessaries of life. But ignorant men seldom appreciate the benefits bestowed upon them by others ; only the educated are obedient and thoughtful. When the children of Israel came to Marah, they could not drink the bitter waters of that place, and began, for this reason, to murmur against Moses. Moses cast a piece of wood into the water and the water was at once made sweet.

Some time afterwards, when the Israelites were without food, they murmured against Moses and Aaron, and wished themselves back to the flesh-pots and the bread of Egypt. Then said Moses unto them : "Why do you murmur against me and Aaron ? Is it not God that brought you out from Egypt? But trust in Him and He will help you!" On the following morning, the dew covered the surface of the desert, and when it was gone, " there lay a small round thing, as small as the hoar frost upon the ground." When the children of Israel saw it, they asked one another : "What is that? (מַן הוּא) Moses replied to them : "This is the heavenly bread which God had given you to eat

Gather it every morning except on Sabbath; let none leave his house on the Sabbath day to gather it, for it will not be found; but on the sixth day, let every man gather twice as much as on any other day." With this bread, which the Israelites called *Manna*, they were fed forty years, and Aaron took a pot full of it and kept it in the Sanctuary for a perpetual memorial of the provident goodness of God.

Shortly afterwards, the Israelites murmured again against Moses, saying: "Who shall give us *flesh* to eat? We remember the fish which we did eat in Egypt freely, the cucumbers, and the melons, and the leeks, and the onions, and the garlic. But now our soul is dried away; there is nothing at all, besides this Manna, before our eyes." When Moses heard these words he was sorely grieved. But God spoke to him, saying: "Ye shall get flesh to eat, not for one day, not for two days, not for five days, nor for ten days, nor for twenty days; but even a whole month, until it come out of your nostrils, and it be loathsome unto you." Moses could not conceive the possibility of such a help, and said: "The people among whom I am, are six hundred thousand footmen; and Thou hast said: 'I will give them flesh, that they may eat a whole month.' Shall the flocks and the herds be slain for them, to suffice them? Or shall all the fish of the sea be gathered together for them, to suffice them?" And the Eternal said to Moses: "Is the hand of the Eternal waxed too short? Thou shalt see now whether my word shalt come to pass unto thee or not." God then sent a wind which brought quails from the sea in such large numbers that they lay two cubits high upon the ground. And the people gathered them all that day, and all that night, and all the next day, and dried them round about the camp. But many who seized the quails too greedily and ate too great a number of them, died in consequence of their intemperance, and were buried in that place, which received the name *Kibroth-hattaavah,* (*the Graves of Lust.*)

On another occasion, the Israelites suffered from *want of water,* and murmured against Moses, saying: "Would God that we had died in Egypt. Why have ye brought us into this wilderness, where neither figs, no vines, nor pomegranates grow, where there is not even water to drink, and we and our cattle must die?" At the command of God, Moses gathered all the Israelites, brought them before a rock, took his rod, smote the rock twice with it, and the water gushed forth in great abundance, so that·the people could drink to their heart's content.

At some other time, the Israelites were visited also by *serpents*. Moses prayed to God in behalf of the people, and the Eternal informed him how to remove the evil. Moses made a serpent of brass, suspended it upon a pole, and every one who looked upwards towards this serpent of brass—looked up to God—was saved.

---

§ 36.   DIFFICULTIES ARISING FROM REBELLIONS OF INDIVIDUAL ISRAELITES

Not alone the whole people often manifested their discontent and rebellious spirit during their sojourn in the desert, but even individual Israelites of high rank grossly sinned against God and Moses.

Korah, Dathan, Abiram, with two hundred and fifty other Israelites, dissatisfied with the distribution of the offices, entered into a conspiracy against Moses and Aaron, saying: "Wherefore lift ye up yourselves above the congregation of the Eternal? The whole congregation is *holy;* why then do you presume to be better than the rest? Moses stepped up to them and endeavored to pacify them by soft words. But in vain. Then a fire came from heaven and consumed these two hundred and fifty men, while the earth opened and swallowed alive Korah and the other ringleaders. When the Israelites saw this, they cried aloud and fled. But the next morning, they again murmured against Moses and Aaron, for they thought that these had caused the death of the rebels. This renewed rebellion brought upon them a destructive pestilence, which carried away fourteen thousand seven hundred persons. Aaron went quickly among the congregation, with the censer in his hand, to propitiate God, and. thus stay the ravages of the pestilence. Hereupon God confirmed Aaron, by means of the following miracle, in his office as high·

priest. Moses commanded that thirteen rods, one for each tribe, with the names of the several princes of the tribes inscribed upon them, should be laid up in the tabernacle, that of the tribe of Levi bearing the name of Aaron. On the following morning it was discovered that Aaron's rod alone budded, bloomed, and yielded almonds. The Israelites perceived from this sign that Aaron was the chosen high-priest of the Eternal. Henceforth, the rod of Aaron was kept near the Ark of the Covenant, as a perpetual warning for the rebels.

At some other time, even Aaron and Miriam spoke against Moses, because he had married a stranger, saying: "God speaketh also through us, not alone through Moses." This repugnance of the nearest relatives of Moses provoked the wrath of God, who said: "are ye not afraid to speak against my faithful servant Moses?" and Miriam was immediately punished with leprosy. When Aaron saw her, he became afraid and implored Moses for forgiveness, both in his own and his sister's behalf. Moses prayed to God for her, and God pardoned her; but she was shut out from the camp seven days, and then only she was received in again.

The law concerning the Sabbath was deemed too heavy a burden by several Israelites. In spite of God's prohibition, some went out on that day to gather Manna. Moses reproached them, saying: "How long do you refuse to keep God's commandments? Behold! the Eternal hath given you the Sabbath, therefore He giveth you on the sixth day the bread for two days." Another man, however, who was found gathering *wood* on the Sabbath day, was stoned to death, at the command of God, without the camp, before the whole congregation.

§ 37. Wars with Neighboring Nations.

Shortly after the Israelites had entered the wilderness, they were attacked by the *Amalekites*. Moses intrusted the command in this struggle to his gallant and faithful servant *Joshua*. He himself went upon a hill and uplifted his hands in fervent prayer to God. The Israelites having

Moses all the time before their eyes, felt inspired for the contest, and fought bravely and victoriously, as long as they beheld his hands raised towards heaven. When the victory was gained, Moses erected an altar and called it: *" God (is) my banner !"*

Jethro, Moses' father-in-law, having heard of this victory and all the miracles which God had wrought through Moses, went with Zipporah, the wife of Moses, and their two sons, to the camp of the Israelites. Moses rejoiced at their arrival, brought them into his tent, told Jethro all that God had already done for his people. Jethro deeply moved by the narrative, exclaimed: "Now I know that the Eternal is mightier than all the gods. On the following day, Moses sat to judge the people from morning unto the evening. When Jethro saw this, he said to him: "The thing that thou doest is not good. Thou wilt surely wear away, both thou and the people; for this thing is too heavy for thee ; thou art not able to perform it thyself alone. Follow my counsel : teach the people good laws and ordinances, and show them distinctly what they should do. Moreover, provide out of all the people, able and honest men, who fear God, men of truth and hating selfishness. Make these rulers over thousands, over hundreds, over fifties, and over tens, and let only the *most important* matters be brought before thyself." Moses obeyed the advice of his father-in-law, and shortly afterwards dismissed him again to his own home.

When the Israelites, after wandering forty years through the desert, approached the land of *Edom*, which was inhabited by the descendants of Esau, Moses sent messengers to their king, with the request to let Israel pass through his country. But this request was rudely and abruptly refused. Now the Israelites showed themselves more generous ; they did not attack them, not willing, as the Edomites were related to them, to shed the blood of their brethren, but moved toward Mount *Hor*, where Aaron died, being 123 years old, and was bewailed and mourned over by the whole people of Israel.

But the *Amorites* and their king, *Sihon*, were not treated in the same generous manner by the Israelites. When they, too, would not permit them to pass peaceably through their country, they attacked the Israelites, and the latter were compelled, in self-defence, to make war upon them, defeated them, and took possession of their land. *Og*, King of *Bashan*, who acted in the same manner as the King of the Amorites, brought the same destruction upon his nation. The lands of these kings were afterwards assigned to the tribes of *Reuben* and *Gad* and *half* the tribe of *Manasseh*, under the condition however, that they should go with their brethren over the Jordan and assist them in the conquest of Canaan. Near the boundary of this country, Moses and Eleazar, who had succeeded his father Aaron in the office of high-priest, numbered the people, the men from twenty years old and upward—with the exception of the tribe of Levi, which, comprising the priests and ministers of God, received no portion at the division of the land of Canaan—and found that there were six hundred and one thousand seven hundred and thirty men who could bear arms, none of whom, with the exception of *Joshua* and *Caleb*, were amongst those that Moses and Aaron had mustered in the wilderness of *Sinai*.

The fate of the Amorites greatly alarmed *Balak*, King of *Moab*, when he saw the approach of the numerous host of the Israelites. In this dread, he sent to a distant country for *Balaam*, a renowned sorcerer, and requested him to curse Israel, for he believed that the curse of this man would be fulfilled. The messengers of the king came to Balaam with precious gifts; but when he refused to comply with the request of Balak, other messengers of still higher rank, and bearing still more precious gifts were sent. Balaam again refused; yet, on the following morning he at last consented and departed with them. When Balak heard that Balaam was coming, he went forth to meet him, and then led him to a high eminence, whence he could see the whole camp of the Israelites. Here Balaam caused the king to build altars and offer sacrifices. Instead, however, as it was expected, of pronouncing the curse, Balaam blessed Israel. Balak then led him upon another eminence; but he again pronounced a benediction. And when the king led the sorcerer upon a third eminence, a third blessing was pronounced. "For," said Balaam, "the word that God hath put in my mouth, that

I have spoken." Afterwards Israel became involved in a war with the Midionites, and the latter were defeated, and their land taken. Amongst the slain was also Balaam the sorcerer.

§ 38. MOSES SENDS SPIES INTO CANAAN. THE CLOSE OF ISRAEL'S WANDERINGS IN THE WILDERNESS.

In the second year after the exodus from Egypt, Moses sent spies to Canaan, that they might explore the land and report to the Israelites both with regard to its inhabitants and its fruitfulness. Twelve men, one from every tribe, departed upon this expedition. After the lapse of forty days, they returned, and reported as follows: "The land which we have explored is good and fruitful: behold these fruits which we have brought thence"—pointing to a large cluster of grapes and other fruits—"it is a land that floweth, as it were, with milk and honey. But its inhabitants are giants, compared with whom we are like grasshoppers." Upon hearing these words, the people became greatly alarmed, cried aloud and wept the whole night. Joshua and Caleb, who were among the spies, contradicted the report of their companions, and addressed the people, saying: "Only rebel not ye against the Eternal, neither fear ye the people of the land, for they are like bread for us." But the Israelites would not listen to them, attempted even to stone the speakers to death, and resolved to elect a chief, and to return to Egypt. But the Lord suddenly appeared and said unto Moses: "How long will this people provoke me? And how long will it be ere they believe me, notwithstanding all the signs which I have wrought among them? I will smite them with the pestilence and utterly destroy them, and will make of thee a greater nation and mightier than Israel is." Now, upon this occasion Moses manifested his sublime virtues and his love for his people. *His* happiness was of the least concern to him; the imminent danger of the destruction of his people filled him with profound grief, and he implored God to pardon their iniquity. Then said the Lord: "I have pardoned according to thy word. But as truly as I live, all those men who have seen my miracles which I did in

Egypt and in the wilderness, and have tempted me now these ten times, and have not hearkened to my voice, surely they shall not see the land which I swore unto their fathers, the land of Canaan, but they shall all die in the wilderness; but unto their children I shall give it for an inheritance. After the number of the days in which the land was searched, ye shall atone for your iniquities forty years, and wander about in the desert. Only *Joshua* and Caleb, because they have clung faithfully to me, they shall come into the promised land." Moses communicated these words to the people, and they mourned greatly.

Shortly before the close of these forty years, the Israelites came into the wilderness of *Zin*, where Miriam died and was buried.

---

§ 39. Moses' Farewell Address to his People. His Death. [Deuteronomy i.-xxxv.]

When the forty years were drawing to their close, and the time approached that Moses was to die, he assembled the whole people, and publicly and solemnly admonished them never to depart from the law of God. "Ye shall add nothing to it," he continued, "nor diminish aught from it, but observe the commandments of the Eternal your God. *For this is your wisdom and your understanding in the sight of the nations, which shall hear all these statutes and say:* ' SURELY THIS GREAT NATION IS A WISE AND UNDERSTANDING PEOPLE.' For what nation is there so great, to which God is nigh, as the Lord our God in all things for which we call unto him? And what nation is there so great, that hath statutes and judgments so *righteous* as all these laws, which I set before you this day? Therefore, forget not what ye have heard and seen, but relate it unto your children, and your children's children. Specially remember the day that ye stood before God on Sinai, where the Lord spoke unto you out of the midst of the fire and the clouds. For ask of the days that are past, whether there hath ever been a people that heard the voice of God as ye have heard; or whether God hath ever chosen for himself a nation like yourselves, by so

many wonders, and by war, and by so mighty a hand?
Thou hast seen it, that thou mightest know: THE LORD BE
YOUR GOD, AND THERE IS NONE BESIDES HIM! *The Lord
hath chosen you, not because ye were more in number than
any people, for ye were the fewest of all people: but because
the Eternal loved you, and because He would keep the oath
which He had sworn unto your fathers.* And forget not
the way which He led you these forty years, and gave you
bread to eat, and water to drink in the wilderness. Behold! the heaven and the heaven of heavens are the Lord's
thy God, and the earth also with all that therein is, and
yet He hath chosen you to be His peculiar people. Therefore, be no more stiff-necked. The Lord your God is Lord
of Lords, a great God, mighty and terrible, who regardeth
not persons, nor taketh reward; who doth execute the
judgment of the fatherless and widow, and loveth the
stranger, I call heaven and earth to witness this day
against you, that I have set before you life and death, a
blessing, if you obey the commandments of God, and a
curse, if you do not obey." And Moses said furthermore
to the children of Israel: "I am hundred and twenty years
old this day; I can no more go out and come in. Joshua,
he shall henceforth be your leader. Fear not, the Lord
will ever watch over you: He will not fail you, nor forsake you." Moses then called unto Joshua, and said unto
him, in the sight of all Israel: "Be strong and of good
courage. Thou shalt bring this people into the promised
land, and divide it among the tribes. Fear not, nor be
dismayed; the Lord will be with thee, He will not forsake
thee." Hereupon Moses delivered the book of the law,
which he had written, unto the priests, and said to them:
"Take this book of the law, and put it in the side of the
Ark of the Covenant of the Lord your God, and at the end
of every seven years, in the solemnity of the year of release, on the Feast of Tabernacles, ye shall read this law
before all Israel in their hearing." Having closed this
speech, Moses recited a song which he had written, and
left it to the Israelites for a memento, took leave from the
tribes of his people, blessed them, and went up from the
plains of Moab to the Mountain of *Nebo*, to the top of
Pisgah, that is over against Jericho. There the Eternal

showed him the whole land of Canaan, and said: "This is the land which I have sworn unto the descendants of Abraham, Isaac and Jacob. I have caused thee to see it with thine eyes, but thou shalt not go over thither." The sight of the beautiful land filled the soul of the great prophet with delight; he thanked God for the love shown unto his people, closed his eyes, and fell asleep to awake in the promised land of eternity. Such is the death of the champion of Virtue; his last thoughts are engaged with the happiness of his beloved ones—his last wish is the salvation of mankind.

Moses was one hundred and twenty years old when he died; his eye was not dim, nor his natural strength abated. There arose no other prophet like Moses, who knew God so clearly, and to whom God so often and so manifestly revealed Himself. He was buried in the valley near the mountain where he died, but no man knows the place of his grave, even to this day.

IV.

ISRAEL AS A NATION.

A. Joshua.—The Judges.

---

§ 40. JOSHUA.—THE CONQUEST OF CANAAN.   [The Book of Joshua i.]   2533 A.M.

GOD'S promise to give the Israelites the land of Canaan, was now brought to its fulfillment. After the death of Moses, God said to *Joshua*, the disciple and chosen successor of the great prophet, and who was a better warrior than his master : " My servant Moses is dead ; now therefore, arise, go over this Jordan, thou and all this people, unto the land which I give to you. As I was with Moses, so I will be with thee. Be strong and of good courage, and let this book of the law not depart from thy mouth ; *do not depart from the law of Moses, either to the right hand or to the left ;* then thou shalt have success in all that thou undertakest." Joshua at once made ready, together with his people to march upon Canaan. Prudent as he was, he sent, before he marched forth, two men as spies into the land, to survey it. When they returned with favorable and encouraging reports, he broke up with his people to invade Canaan. On the opposite side of Jordan he erected a monument of twelve stones, in commemoration of his happy passage over the river, and then continued his march towards *Jericho.* Jericho was so strongly fortified, that no one could go in or come out. But God gave this city into the hands of the Israelites without battle ; its inhabitants were put to death, and all their silver and gold, and vessels of brass and iron were consecrated unto God. *Achan,* who had secretly taken some of the booty to himself, was stoned to death for this trespass.

The Israelites then marched upon *Ai* and captured also this city. After the capture of Ai, Joshua erected an altar on Mount *Ebal*, and read the whole law before the people. There was not a word of all that Moses had commanded which Joshua did not fulfill. The Levites spoke with a loud voice before all the people: "Cursed be the man that maketh any idol and worshipped it!" and all the people said, "Amen!" "Cursed be he that disgraceth his father or mother!" and all the people said: "Amen!" "Cursed be he that removeth his neighbor's land-mark!" and the whole people said, "Amen!" "Cursed be he that maketh the blind to lose his way!" and all the people said, "Amen!" "Cursed be the man that perverteth the judgment of the stranger, the fatherless and the widow!" and all the people said, "Amen!"

Hereupon, the war, which the Israelites carried on with great courage and bravery, was continued seven years, during which they conquered thirty small kingdoms. The inhabitants of Canaan, with whom God was greatly displeased on account of their sins and idolatry, resisted in vain with all the strength of despair; they were defeated, and either fell during the contest, or were compelled to flee and seek another home. The small tribe of the *Gibeonites* escaped by a cunning stratagem. Some men with torn shoes and mouldy bread appeared before Joshua, describing themselves as coming from a far distant country, and imploring him to make a treaty of peace with them. Joshua, regarding their garments and whole conduct as a confirmation of their words, unhesitatingly complied with their request, and concluded with them a treaty of peace. But soon he found that he had been imposed upon, those men proving to have been sent by the Gibeonites. Nevertheless, he did not treat them as enemies, but kept his oath sacred. Moreover, when the Gibeonites were attacked by five neighboring princes, the Israelites, faithful to their treaty, came to their aid, and defeated their enemies.

Joshua made also arrangements with the view of preserving the ceremonial observances connected with divine worship, as prescribed by the law of Moses. He introduced the general observance of the Covenant of Abraham, and celebrated the Passover Festivals. After seven years of warfare he divided the land, both the conquered and the unconquered portions thereof, among the nine and a half tribes, leaving to each tribe to conquer the rest belonging to him. The tribe of Levi had forty-eight cities assigned to them, as they lay scattered over the territories of the other tribes.

§ 41. Joshua's Parting Address—His Death.
[Book of Joshua, xxiii. xxiv.]

After a long time of rest in the land of Israel, when Joshua felt that his end was approaching, he assembled the chiefs of Israel, together with all the people, around him, and said to them: "I am old, and soon shall go the way of all the earth. But be ye courageous, and consider that the Lord left not *one* word unfulfilled of all that He had promised unto us through Moses. But, as all good things are come upon you which the Lord promised you, so shall He bring upon you all the *evil things*, when ye have transgressed the covenant of God and served other gods. Now, therefore, keep and do all that is written in the Book of the Law, that ye turn not aside therefrom, either to the right hand or to the left."

Shortly afterwards, Joshua assembled the people once more at *Shechem*, and said unto them: "God has given you a land which ye have not tilled, and cities which ye built not, and vine-yards and olive-yards which ye planted not. Now, therefore, be thankful to the Lord, fear Him, and serve Him in sincerity and in truth. But if it seem evil to you to serve the Lord, choose you this day whom you will serve; but as for me and my house, we will serve the Lord." And the people answered: "God forbid that we should forsake the Lord; we also will serve the Lord, for He is our God." Then said Joshua to the people: "You cannot serve the Lord and strange gods, for the Lord is a holy and jealous God: He will not forgive your transgressions, nor your sins." The people answered again, saying: "Nay, but we will serve the Lord." Then said

Joshua: "You are witness against yourselves that you have chosen the Lord to serve Him." They answered: "We are witnesses!" Whereupon Joshua said to them: "Now, therefore, put away the strange gods that are among you, and henceforth incline your heart unto the Lord God of Israel alone." The people exclaimed: "The Lord our God will we serve, and his voice we will obey!" And they fulfilled their vow as long as Joshua lived, and also some time afterwards, during the days of the Elders that overlived him. He wrote all these things in a book of law, took a great stone, and set it up there under an oak near the Sanctuary of the Lord for a memorial. He then dismissed them, every man to his inheritance.

Shortly afterwards he died at the age of a hundred and ten years, and was buried in the mount of Ephraim. But the bones of Joseph, which the Israelites had brought up from Egypt, they buried in Shechem, in a parcel of ground which Jacob had bought.

42. THE JUDGES. [Book of the Judges.]

After the death of Joshua, the Israelites had no longer a common chief. There was no *unity* among the several tribes. While each of them attended to its own affairs, they weakened each other by bloody civil wars. They forgot the benefits which God had shown to their forefathers, and weary of the strict laws of Moses, intermarried with the heathens that had been permitted to remain in the country, and thus were led astray to adopt their manner, vices, and idolatrous practices. On account of these aberrations, God forsook them. Whenever they did evil, He delivered them into the hand of their enemies, by whom they were heavily oppressed. Whenever they returned from their sinful ways, God awakened inspired and enlightened men among them, to lead them to victory over their enemies. These men did not only procure for them peace from external enemies, but also—at least many of them—strove to preserve in their midst the belief in the living God. These men were called JUDGES, (*Shophetim*,) because they vindicated the rights of their people against their enemies; and some of them filled moreover, the highest judicial offices in their domes ie affairs, (*Deborah, Samuel.*) Holy Writ enumerates fifteen of these Judges, who ruled during more than three hundred years over Israel, and mentions their names in the following order: 1, *Othniel;* 2, *Ehud;* 3, *Shamgar;* 4, *Barak* and *Deborah;* 5, *Gideon;* 6, *Abimelech;* 7, *Tolah;* 8, *Jair;* 9, *Jephtah;* 10, *Ibzan;* 11, *Elon;* 12, *Abdon;* 13, *Samson;* 14, *Eli;* 15, *Samuel.*

The first judge over Israel was *Othniel.* He delivered the Israelites from the hand of the Mesopotamian king, whereupon the land enjoyed peace for forty years. After the death of Othniel, the Israelites again did evil, and the Lord punished them by giving them up for eighteen years, to the power of the king of the Moabites. They prayed to God for help from their misery, and he inspired *Ehud* to be their deliverer, who procured them peace and tranquility for eighty years. He was succeeded by *Shamgar,* who defeated the Philistines and thus liberated the Israelites from their enemies. But soon the Israelites again forgot their God, in punishment for which they were given up to the oppression of *Jabin,* king of Hazor, for twenty years. When the Israelites repented and cried unto the Lord, He inspired *Deborah,* a pious woman, to become their deliverer. She urged upon *Barak,* in the name of God to make war upon the enemy, and marched herself at the head of the Israelitish army to the battle-field, assisted in putting the Canaanites to flight, and perpetuated this glorious victory by a hymn of praise and thanks, which she composed and sang, together with Barak, after the battle, in glorification of the Lord.

------

§ 43. The Judges. (Continued.)

After the lapse of several years, the Israelites again did evil in the sight of God, wherefore he delivered them over into the hands of the Midianites for seven years. At that time, there lived a man in Israel, *Gideon,* of the tribe of Manassoh, surnamed *Jerubbaal,* from his struggle against the idolatrous worship of Baal. God appointed him to be the deliverer of the Israelites, when they cried unto Him for help. Gideon was just thrashing wheat in a wine-press, to hide it from the Midianites who swept over the land as grasshoppers and laid it waste, so that the Israel-ites had almost nothing left whereon to live, when he re-solved to break the heavy yoke which the strangers had laid upon his nation. When the Midianites came again into the land to devastate it, he marched against them with an army of thirty-two thousand men. But God said to him: "The people that are with thee, are too many for me to give the Midianites into their hands, lest Israel vaunt themselves against me, saying, *Our own* hand have saved us. Now, therefore, proclaim in the ears of the peo-ple, saying, Whosoever is fearful and afraid, let him return to his home! And there returned twenty-two thousand men. But God continued, saying: "The people are yet too many." Hereupon Gideon retained only three hundred men. During the night, God said to him: "Go down into the valley where the enemies have pitched their tents." When Gideon arrived there, he saw men and camels with-out number, and heard a Midianite speak to his fellow, saying: "Behold, I have just dreamed that a cake of barley bread had come into the tent and overturned it." "This means nothing else," replied the other, "than that we shall be defeated by Gideon." When Gideon heard these speeches, he thanked God and returned to his men full of joy. divided them into three companies, and gave every one a trumpet into one hand, and a pitcher with a lamp in it into the other. He then said to them: "Now look on me, and do as I shall do; when I blow with a trumpet, then blow ye the trumpets also, and cry, The sword of the Lord and of Gideon!" The men did as he had directed them, and the whole army of the enemy became so panic-stricken and confused that they took to flight and did not even venture to turn their heads. Gideon pursued and slew them. After this victory, the Israelites again enjoyed peace for forty years. In gratitude for their delivery by Gideon, the Israelites offered him the heredit-ary rule over them, but he refused to accept it, and pre-ferred a quiet life in his native city. But after his death, his son *Abimelech* aspired to the rule, which his father had rejected, and slew, to accomplish his object, his seventy brothers on one stone. Only the youngest of Gideon's sons, *Jotham*, escaped. He went upon the summit of Mount *Gerizim*, lifted up his voice and exclaimed: "Hearken unto me, ye men of Shechem, that God may hearken unto you. The trees went forth on a time to anoint a king over them; and they said unto the olive tree, Reign thou over us. But the olive tree said unto them, Should I leave my fatness, wherewith by me they honor God and man, and go to be promoted over the trees? And the trees said to the fig-tree, Come thou, and reign over us. But the fig-tree said unto them, Should I forsake my sweetness, and my good fruit, and go to be promoted over the trees? Then said the trees unto the vine, Come thou, and reign over us. And the vine said unto them, Should I leave my wine, which cheereth God and man, and go to be promoted over the trees? Then said all the trees unto the bramble, Come thou and reign over us. And the bramble said unto the trees, If in truth ye anoint me king over you, then come and put your trust in my shadow; and if not, let fire come out of the bramble, and devour the cedars of Lebanon. Now, therefore, if ye have done truly and sincerely, in that ye have made Abimelech king, and if ye have dealt well with Jerubbaal and his house, and have done unto him according to the deserving of his hands; (for my father fought for you, and adventured his life far, and delivered you out of the hand of Midian: And ye are risen up against my father's house this day, and have slain his sons. threescore and ten persons, upon one stone, and have made Abimelech, the son of his maid-servant, king over the men of Shechem, because he is your brother;) if ye then have dealt truly and sincerely with Jerubbaal and with his house this day, then rejoice ye in Abimelech, and let him also rejoice in you: but if not, let fire come out from Abimelech, and devour the men of Shechem, and the house of Millo; and let fire come out from the men of Shechem. and from the house of Millo. and devour Abimelech." After finishing this speech *Jotham* fled to a distant region of the country.

Abimelech had reigned not more than three years, when discord arose between him and the people of Shechem.

the same who had raised him to the office of Judge. *Gaal*, the son of Ebed, and his brothers went about in Shechem and conspired against him, saying: "Who are we, and who is Abimelech, that we should serve him? If I were your ruler, I should remove him." When Abime-lech heard of this, he, gathered his people, took Shechem, slew its inhabitants, and destroyed the city. He set also fire to the *tower* (citadel) of Shechem, and thus caused the death of those that had taken refuge therein. But when he attempted to burn also the tower of *Thebez*, together with the people that had fled into it, God revealed His unfailing justice: "a woman cast a piece of a mill-stone upon his head, which broke his skull. Then he called hastily unto the young man his armor-bearer, and said unto him, Draw thy sword and slay me, that men say not of me, A woman slew him. And the young man thrust him through, and he died." Now, when his men saw that he was dead, they departed, every man to his home.

After Abimelech, *Tola* and *Jair* were successively Judges in Israel. When the Israelites again followed the paths of sin and iniquity, God delivered them over to the power of the *Ammonites*. Then the elders of Gilead went to *Jephtah*, a valiant and mighty fellow-citizen of theirs, whom they had expelled from their city, and entreated him to be their captain in the war with the Ammonites. But he said to them: "Did not ye hate me, and expel me out of my father's house? And why are ye come unto me now when ye are in distress?" The elders replied: "Therefore we turn again to thee now, that thou mayest go with us and fight against the children of Ammon, and afterwards be our chief." Then Jephtah went with the elders, and the people made him their captain and leader. Before, however, he went to war, he sent messengers to the king of the Ammonites, to demand of him to desist from his hostilities. But when the king would not com-ply with the demand, Jephtah prepared for war. Before engaging in battle, he made a vow, saying: "If God will grant me a victory over our enemies, then it shall be, that whatever cometh forth of the doors of my house to meet me first when I return in peace from the children of Ammon, shall surely be consecrated unto the Lord! I will offer it up for a burnt offering." Jephtah gained t' e victory, and when he returned to his home, behold! his only daughter and child came out to meet him with timbrels and with dances. When he saw her, he rent his clothes and exclaimed: "Alas! my daughter! thou hast brought me very low, and causest me deep grief of the heart, for I have made a vow unto the Lord, and I can not recall it." Then she said: "Do as thou hast vowed. But one thing, I pray thee, do for me: Let me alone but two months, that I may go into the mountains and bewail, with my playmates, the sad fate that now awaits me." Her father granted her request, and then performed his vow. Jephtah was six years Judge over Israel. His successors were *Ibzan, Elon, Abdon,* and the strong *Samson.*

§ 44. The History of Sampson. [Book of the Judges xiii.-xvi.]

There lived a man in *Zorah,* named *Manoah,* who had no children. At last an angel of God announced to him the birth of a son, that should become the deliverer of the Israelites from the hands of the Philistines, who, at that time oppressed them most severely. His wife afterwards bare him a son, as the angel had foretold him, and he called him *Samson.* His parents resolved that he should be consecrated to God, that is, become a Nazarite: no razor should come on his head, he should not be permitted to drink wine or any other strong beverage, or eat any thing unclean, throughout his life. When Samson had reached the age of manhood, he went to Timnath, a city of the Philistines. Here he saw a Philistine maiden with whom he was so much pleased, that he requested his parents to get her for him as his wife. But they said to him: "Is there no woman among the daughters of thy relatives, or among all thy people, that thou shouldest go to take a wife of the heathen Philistines? But Samson insisted upon his request, saying: "Get *her* for me, for she pleaseth me well" This marriage, he thought, would afford him opportunity to reward the Philistines for the heavy oppression under which they made the Israelites to suffer. After some time when Samson went down to Timnath with his parents, he met a young lion and rent him, with his bare hands, as he would have rent a kid. A few days after, he found a swarm of bees and honey in the carcass of the lion. He took thereof, ate it, and brought some of it also to his parents.

When his nuptial feast was celebrated, Samson said to his thirty Philistinian companions: "I will now put forth a riddle to you; if ye can solve it within the seven days of the feast, then I will give you thirty shirts and thirty festival garments; but if you can not solve it, then you shall give me thirty shirts and thirty festival garments." They replied: "Put forth thy riddle, that we may hear it." Then said Samson: "Out of the eater came forth meat, and out of the strong came forth sweetness," After having in vain attempted, for three days, to solve the riddle, the young men went to his wife and threatened to set the house of her father on fire, if she did not entice her husband to tell her the solution. Hereupon Samson's wife wept a long time before him, until he told her the solution, which she communicated to his companions. Angry at this, he went out and slew thirty Philistines, took their garments and gave them to the young men. Then he returned to his parents, leaving his wife with her father. In the mean while, her parents married her to another man, which afforded Samson a just cause for an attack upon the Philistines.

Having returned, some time afterward, to Timnath, his father-in-law would not admit him into his house, saying: "I thought indeed that thou hadst utterly hated her, therefore I gave her to another man." Burning with anger, on account of this treatment, Samson went and caught three hundred foxes, coupled them together by their tails, took torches and put one of them in the midst between each couple of the foxes, tied to their tails. He then set the torches on fire, and let the foxes loose into the corn-fields of the Philistines, so that their entire crop was burned down. In revenge for this, the Philistines burned his wife and her father to death. This deed Samson avenged likewise by a greater slaughter among the

Philistines. After this, he went into the desert of Judah, and dwelt in the top of the rock Etam. The Philistines then marche 1 forth and pitched their tents in Judah. To avert all danger, the men of Judah delivered Samson bound into their hands. But as soon as he was in the midst of his enemies, he burst the cords that were upon his arms as flax, took a fresh jaw-bone of an ass and slew one thousand men therewith. Soon after this he went to *Gaza.* The inhabitants of this city laid wait for him all night, to kill him. But about midnight he rose, seized the doors of the gate of the city, raised them from their hinges, put them upon his shoulders, and carried them upon the top of a mountain.

After that, he loved a woman in the valley of *Sorek,* whose name was *Delilah.* The Philistines went to her with the request to find out the secret of his extraordinary strength, and promised her rich rewards if she should succeed. Upon her question to Samson, wherein his strength consisted, he replied: "If they bind me with seven green withs that were never dried, then I shall be weak." When Delilah bound him with such withs, he burst them as a thread. Then said Delilah: "Behold, thou hast mocked me; now tell me, I pray thee, wherewith thou mightest be bound." He replied: "If they bind me fast with new ropes, then shall I be weak." And Delilah bound him with new ropes, but he tore them from his arm like a thread. When Delilah saw this, she said to him thou hast again mocked me; tell me, I pray thee, wherein thou mightest be bound." And he said: "If thou weavest the seven locks of my head with the web, then I shall be weak." But she found herself again deceived. Now she said to him: "How canst thou say, I love thee, when thou art not sincere toward me?" Now, when she pressed him daily in this manner, he at last yielded and told her, that he would lose all his strength if his hair should be cut. When Delilah saw that he had opened his heart to her, she made him sleep upon her knees, called for a man, and caused him to shave off the seven locks of Samson's head. Then she exclaimed: "The Philistines upon thee, Samson!" He awoke and tried to out as at other times, and shake himself, but soon found that his strength was departed. The Philistines took him, bound him, put out his eyes, and carried him to *Gaza*, to grind the mill in the prison house.

When, some time after, the Philistines celebrated a feast in the temple of their idol *Dagon*, they sent for Sampson, that he might afford them sport, and thus heighten their joy. But Sampson, feeling that his hair had grown again, and his strength returned, called unto God, and prayed: "O Lord! remember me, I pray Thee, and strengthen me, I pray Thee, only this once!" Then he took hold of the middle pillars upon which the house stood, and bent them with all his strength, exclaiming: "*Let Samson die with the Philistines!*" and the whole building fell upon the lords and the people gathered therein, so that all were buried under its ruins, together with Samson. His brethren and the whole household of his father came down and took his body, and buried him in the burying-place of his father.

§ 45. ELI AND SAMUEL. [1 Samuel i.-iv.]

Eli was one before the last of the Judges, and at the same time Priest at *Shiloh*, where the Ark of the Covenant stood. Pious Israelites used to go there to offer sacrifices to God and to thank Him for His blessings. Amongst these pious worshippers were also a man named *Elkanah*, and his wife *Hannah*, who went to Shiloh every year. Hannah was deeply grieved and wept, because she had no children; even the friendly words of her husband could not comfort her. Once she entered the House of God weeping, and prayed in the following manner: "O Lord of hosts! behold the affliction of Thy handmaid! Give unto me I pray Thee, a son, and I will give him unto Thee: he shall be consecrated unto Thee all the days of his life." While she thus prayed to God she was observed by Eli, who thought she was drunk, because he saw only her lips move, while her voice was not heard. And he said to her: "How long wilt thou be drunken?" Hannah answered, and said: "No, my lord, I am a woman of a sorrowful spirit; I have drunk neither wine nor strong

drink, but have poured out my soul before the Lord."
Then Eli answered, and said: "Go in peace; and the God
of Israel grant thee thy petition that thou hast asked of
Him." Filled with cheerful courage, she returned home,
ate and drank again, and was no longer sad. God had
hearkened to her prayer: she had soon a son, whom she
called *Samuel*.

When she had weaned her son, she took him to Eli,
and said: "My lord, I am the woman that stood by thee
here. praying unto the Lord.—For this child I prayed, and
the Lord hath granted me my petition which I asked of
Him: therefore also will I perform my vow, and consecrate this child unto the service of God all the days of his
life." Eli took the boy, and trained him unto God-fearing
piety and virtue.

§ 46.   The Sons of Eli.

Eli had two sons, named *Hophni* and *Phineas*, who
were very wicked and mischievous lads. They feared
neither God nor men, disturbed the Israelites in their
pious devotions, stole the flesh of the sacrifices from the
pots, and committed many other abominable excesses.
Now it was the duty of Eli to punish his sons as severely
as possible, for their great misdeeds, but he did not perform this duty; he reproached them, it is true, for their
evil conduct, and admonished them to improve; but they
did not mind the exhortations of their father, who, moreover, was already too old, too feeble and lenient, to inflict
more severe punishment upon them. But young Samuel
was obedient to his teacher, grew very pious and good,
and was in favor with God, and also with men.

God having appointed Samuel for His prophet, revealed
to him His intention severely to punish Eli and his sons,
for the iniquities of his house, the iniquities of his sons.
This revelation was soon fulfilled. A war having broken
out between the Israelites and the Philistines, Eli's sons
marched to the camp with the Ark of the Covenant, that
it might be borne before the Israelitish warriors, and thus,
as it was the symbol of the presence of God, inspire them
with courage. With impatient anxiety did Eli wait

for some intelligence concerning the fate of his people. At last a messenger arrived and said to him: "Israel is fled before the Philistines, and there hath been also a great slaughter among the people, and thy two sons also are dead, and the Ark of God is in the hands of the enemy." When the aged Eli, who was ninety-eight years old, heard this sad intelligence, he was struck with such fright that he fell from his chair, broke his neck and died, after having judged over Israel forty years.

§ 47. The Meritorious Acts of Samuel.

The Philistines placed the Ark of the Lord in the temple of their idol god Dagon. For this profanation God sent a heavy plague upon them, so that their princes determined to return the Ark of the Covenant to the Israelites. Yet, the Israelites still remained in the power of their enemy. Wherefore Samuel resolved to become their deliverer. He assembled the people at *Mizpeh*, and told them what they ought to do, and what alone could be of avail to them. "If you," thus he spoke to them, "do return unto the Lord with all your hearts, serve Him alone faithfully and sincerely, He will again deliver you out of the hand of your enemy." The people loudly confessed their sins, and fasted the whole day with profound repentance. While their trespass-offerings were yet burning upon the altar, the Philistines appeared to fight against them. Samuel prayed to God for his people, and a terrible thunder-storm broke upon the Philistines, which caused such confusion amongst them, that they took to flight. Thus the sincere repentance of the Israelites had proved a greater help to them than their outward worship of the Ark of the Covenant. In memoey of this victory, Samuel took a stone, set it up between Mizpeh and Shen as a grateful memorial, and called it *Eben-ezer*, saying: "Hitherto hath the Lord helped us."

Every one now acknowledged that Samuel was a trustworthy prophet. Under his rule, the affairs of the people improved. He admonished his brethren to remove the strange gods and serve the Lord alone; he employed, in all possible manner, the time of peace for the revival of religious feelings. He travelled about the country to administer justice, and established *Schools of Prophets*, in which pious youths were instructed in Religion. To the very day of his death he lived and labored for the welfare of his people.

---

§ 48.   GOD TRIES AND GUIDES THE PIOUS. [The Book of Ruth.]

In the days of the Judges, there lived a pious woman named *Ruth*. She was a Moabite, and married to a son of *Elimelech*, who had removed, during a famine in Canaan, with his wife *Naomi* and his two sons, into the land of Moab. Soon Elimelech and his two sons died; whereupon, the poor, afflicted wife and mother resolved to return to her native country Canaan, where she could still find some relatives and friends, and recover her lands. Her two daughters-in-law accompanied her a great distance. But the hour of separation at last arrived. The three widows held each other firmly embraced; the memory of their beloved departed ones filled their hearts with grief and sadness; tears gushed forth from their pious eyes; the words died upon their lips. At last the kind mother addressed the following words to her daughters: "Return, I pray you, my daughters; the Lord deal kindly with you as ye have dealt with the dead, and with me." Then she kissed them; and they lifted up their voices, and wept, and they said unto her: "No, no! we will go with thee unto thy people." Now, Naomi entreated them still more urgently, saying: "Nay, my daughters, for it grieveth me much for your sakes. Return to your homes!" *Orpah* now kissed her mother-in-law, and returned; but Ruth clave unto her, and she said: "I cannot leave thee: whithersoever thou goest, I will go; wherever thou lodgest, I will lodge; thy people shall be my people, thy God shall be my God. Where thou diest, will I die, and there will I be buried." Naomi embraced once more her faithful daughter-in-law, and took her with her to Bethlehem.

And when they arrived there, all the city was moved about them, and they said: "Is this Naomi?" And she said unto them: "Call me not Naomi, call me Mara, for the Almighty hath dealt very bitterly with me." But Ruth, still possessed of youthful strength, willingly worked for her mother-in-law; she went out into the fields to glean ears of corn, and thus maintained herself and Naomi. Kind Providence so ordained it that Ruth should glean in the fields of the wealthy Boaz, who was a relative of Naomi. Observing her industry, he asked his reapers, saying: "Who is yonder damsel that gleans so industriously?" They answered: "It is Ruth, the daughter-in-law of Naomi: she has been here ever since early in the morning, gleaning continually. without even looking around." Then Boaz went to her. and said: "Listen, my daughter. Go not to glean in another field, but abide here fast by my maidens. I have charged the young men that they shall not trouble thee, and when thou art athirst, go unto the vessels and drink from them." Then she fell on her face, and said: "Why have I found such grace in thine eyes, although I am a stranger?" Boaz answered, saying: "It hath fully been shown unto me all that thou hast done unto thy mother-in-law. May the Lord reward thee for thy noble deeds!" Thereupon Boaz commanded his young men purposely to let fall some of the ears for her, that her gleanings might be more abundant. Ruth gleaned until evening, beat the corn out, and brought it home to her mother-in-law, besides some portions of her meals which she had reserved for her. When Naomi heard that it was Boaz that had bestowed so much kindness upon her she told Ruth that he was her relative. And Boaz, who became more and more pleased with the industry and correct deportment of Ruth, married her, and was very happy in his wedlock. They had soon a son, whom they called *Obed*. And Naomi enjoyed again a happy life at the house of her daughter-in-law, for which she proved herself grateful. The well-being of Ruth was to her like her own, and she took her child into her lap and became his nurse. This Obed was the grand-father of David

B. The Kings over the Undivided Empire of Israel.

§ 49. SAUL RAISED TO THE ROYAL THRONE. [1 Samuel viii.-xiv.] 2916 A.M.

When Samuel had grown old and felt himself too weak to continue Judge over Israel, he resolved to transfer his office to his sons. But as these were wicked and avaricious men, open to bribery, the people demanded of Samuel, that he should appoint a *king* over them, that they might be ruled as the neighboring nations. This demand caused the displeasure of Samuel. But God said to him.: "Hearken unto the voice of the people, for they have not rejected thee, but they have rejected *me*, that I should no longer reign over them. Now, therefore, hearken unto their voice, yet protest solemnly unto them, and show them the great evil which the rule of a wicked king will produce." In accordance with these words, Samuel addressed the people, saying:

"This will be the manner of the king that shall reign over you: he will take your sons, and appoint them for himself, for his chariots, and to be his horsemen; and some shall run before his chariots.

"And he will appoint him captains over thousands, and captains over fifties; and will set them to ear his ground, and to reap his harvest, and to make his instruments of war, and instruments of his chariots.

"And he will take your daughters to be confectionaries, and to be cooks, and to be bakers.

"And he will take your fields, and your vineyards, and your oliveyards, even the best of them, and give them to his servants.

"And he will take the tenth of your seed, and of your vineyards, and give to his officers, and to his servants.

"And he will take your menservants, and your maid-servants, and your goodliest young men, and your asses, and put them to his work.

"He will take the tenth of your sheep: and ye shall be his servants.

"And ye shall cry out in that day because of your king which ye shall have chosen you; and the Lord will not hear you in that day."

But the people did not heed these representations of Samuel; they insisted upon their demand, saying: "Nay, but we will have a king over us; that we also may be like all the nations, and that our king may judge us, and go out before us, and fight our battles." When Samuel saw that the people would not yield, he said: "Go ye every man to his city." He then anointed, in the name of God, *Saul*, the son of an humble family of the tribe of Benjamin, king over Israel, and presented him as such to the people, who were rejoiced and shouted: "God save the king!" But some discontented and envious men exclaimed: "How shall *this man* save us?" and despised Saul. He. however, pretended not to have heard this remark, and held his peace.

Soon an opportunity presented itself to him, to show himself as a gallant man and the deliverer of his brethren. Having heard that the Ammonites had laid siege to the *Israelitish* city *Jabesh-gilead*, and demanded that the inhabitants should lose their right eyes for a reproach unto all Israel, his indignation was roused, and he took a yoke of oxen, cut them to pieces, and sent these to all the places of Israel, with these words: "Whoever cometh not forth after Saul and after Samuel, so shall it be done unto his oxen." All Israel marched out with one consent against the Ammonites, and defeated them completely. Delighted with this victory, the people exclaimed, saying: "Who are those that said, 'Saul shall not reign over us?' bring the men that we may put them to death." But Saul said: "There shall not a man be put to death this day, for to-day the Lord hath wrought salvation in Israel."

But king Saul did not continue pious and modest; his prosperity made him wicked, so that he did not obey the commands of God on all occasions. During a war with·

the Amalekites, the Lord had commanded him to slay
every living being, and not even to spare their cattle; for
the Amalekites had attacked the Israelites without cause
or reason, during their sojourn in the wilderness, and intended to destroy them.   Contrary to the command of
God, Saul permitted his people to spare the best of the
cattle, and all that was good, and had it offered up for
sacrifices.   Samuel reproached him for this disobedience,
saying: "Behold: to obey is better than sacrifice; disobedience is idolatry.   Because thou hast rejected the word
of the Lord, He hath also rejected thee.   The royal dignity shall be taken from thee; and know, the God of
Israel will not lie nor repent, for He is no man, that He
should repent."   Samuel then turned away from Saul, yet
mourned for him, because God had rejected him.

§ 50.   David anointed King over Israel.   [1 Samuel, xv. xvi. and xvii.]

God said to Samuel: "How long wilt thou mourn for
Saul?   Go to Bethlehem, to *Jesse*, and anoint for me one
of his sons as king over Israel."   Samuel went to the
house of Jesse and had his sons presented to him, that he
might see which of them was the appointed one.   But
God said to him: "Look not upon their countenances, or
on the heighth of their statures; the Lord seeth not as
man seeth; for man looketh upon the outward appearance, but the Lord looketh upon the heart."   Not one of
those presented to him could be anointed.   Whereupon
Jesse sent for his youngest son *David*, who was then
keeping the sheep in the field.   David was of a beautiful
countenance, and, what is still more precious, of a noble
heart.   Now God said to Samuel: "Arise, anoint him,
for *this* is the man!   Then Samuel took the horn of oil,
and anointed him, in the midst of his brethren, as king
over Israel.   From that day David was more and more
filled with the Spirit of the Lord, while Saul became
sadder and sadder and fell into deep melancholy.   David,
who was very skillful in playing the harp, was brought to
the royal court, and cheered Saul, by the tunes of music,

in the hours of his sadness. He became so much endeared to the king, that he made him his armor-bearer.

When the Philistines again came to fight against Saul, a giant by the name of *Goliath* stepped forth from the army of the enemy, and exclaimed, full of pride and haughtiness, saying: "Who ventures to fight with me? If one of you defeat me, then we all will be your servants; but if I defeat him, then shall ye be our servants." When Saul and all Israel heard these words, they became greatly afraid, and no man would venture the contest with the giant. Now it so happened that David was present in the camp, just when Goliath again used that haughty language. He at once said: "I will fight with this giant!" And when his brothers and other Israelites, as well as Saul, attempted to dissuade him from his determination, he answered: "I have already smitten a lion and a bear with my hand; the Lord will deliver me also out of the hand of this Philistine." He then took his shepherd's staff, his sling, and his shepherd's bag filled with smooth stones, and thus went forth to meet the Philistine. When Goliath saw David he disdained him, and said: "Am I a dog that thou comest to me with a staff? Come to me, and I will give thy flesh unto the fowls of the air and to the beasts of the field." David answered and said: *Thou* reliest upon thine own strength, but *I* come in the name of God, whom thou hast defied. Even this day will the Lord deliver thee into my hand, and all the earth shall know that there is a God in Israel." When, at that moment, the giant arose and drew nigh to meet David, the latter took a stone from his bag, slang it, and smote the Philistine in his forehead, so that he fell dead to the ground. David then took the sword of Goliath, and cut off his head therewith. When the Philistines saw that their champion had fallen, they were seized with fear, and driven to flight by the Israelites.

51. SAUL PERSECUTING DAVID. [1 Samuel xviii.-xxiv. xxvi.-xxxi., and 2 Samuel i.]

The victory which David had gained over Goliath, brought glory, happiness, but no less also persecution upon him. Saul took him into his palace, and would no more permit him to return to his native place; he placed him at the head of the army; and Jonathan, the son of Saul, loved him as his own soul, and made a covenant of friendship with him, which he kept most faithfully to the day of his death. But Saul began to be jealous of David; his hatred against him increased every hour, because David was more honored by the people than Saul himself, and he feared that David might become king. One day, while David was playing on the harp before Saul, he cast a javelin at him, but missed him; Saul hereupon removed him from him, and made him his captain over a thousand. But his hatred had not subsided; he incessantly sought opportunities to take the life of David. On one occasion he promised to give him his daughter *Michal* to wife, if he would slay one hundred Philistines. Saul thought that David could never return alive from such a daring expedition; but he was disappointed. David slew two hundred Philistines, and became Saul's son-in-law. The latter, nevertheless, continued to hate him and attempt his life, and would once have indeed succeeded in carrying out his revengeful design, had not Michal saved her husband. But in the same proportion that Saul's hatred against David grew, the love of Jonathan for him grew in strength and fervor. He took care to speak always with the highest praise of David, and endeavored to appease his father. "Let not the king sin against his servant, against David"—thus spoke Jonathan to his father—"because he hath not done the least evil against thee; nay, he hath even risked his life for thee, and slain the Philistines: wherefore then wilt thou sin against innocent blood, to slay David without a cause?"

But these intercessions of Jonathan's produced only a transient effect; Saul's hatred soon awoke again, and Jonathan himself at last advised David no more to return to the king's palace, because he still sought to kill him, but rather to flee and escape.

Upon his flight David came to the city of Nob, to *Ahimelech* the priest, who could not refuse the request of the king's son-in-law, and gave him bread and the sword of Goliath. *Doeg*, an Edomite, and one of Saul's servants who happened to be present, told the king what he had seen. The latter, thinking that Ahimelech was David's ally, caused eighty-five priests to be put to death, and destroyed the whole city.

Thereupon Saul pursued David to the most distant parts of the wilderness; but the latter, conscious of his innocence, confided in God, and found consolation in this confidence, saying: "God is my help, the Lord is the staff of my life; God is with me, I will not fear; what can men do unto me?" About five to six thousand men joined him in his flight from Saul's persecutions, and although several opportunities presented themselves when he could have taken the life of the king, yet he was too noble hearted to take revenge upon his enemy, and too pious to lift his hand against the anointed head of his king. Once Saul pursued him with three thousand men, and having entered a cave near the hiding-place of David, it was an easy matter for the latter to take his life. But the noble fugitive would do him no harm, He secretly cut a piece of the skirt of Saul's robe, and cried unto him: "Behold, my lord and king! the skirt of thy robe in my hand. Know and see that there is neither evil nor transgression in my hand, and that my heart designeth no sin against thee." When Saul heard these words he wept, and said to David: "Thou art more righteous than I. May the Lord reward thee good for that thou hast done unto me this day."

Shortly afterwards, Saul again pursued David in the wilderness of *Ziph*. One night, David entered with *Abishai*, the son of *Zerujah*, the camp of the king, and found him asleep, with his spear stuck in the ground, and a cruse of water near by. At this sight, Abishai said to David: "God hath delivered thine enemy into thy hand this day: now, therefore, let me smite him, I pray thee, with the spear even to the earth at once, so that he need no second blow." But David said: "God forbid that I should stretch forth my hand against the Lord's anointed! but, I pray thee, take thou now the spear that is near his bolster, and the cruse of water, and let us go." Abishai did as David had bidden him; whereupon the latter went up to the top of a hill, and cried to *Abner*, the chief captain of Saul, saying: "Abner, art thou not a man like whom there is no other in Israel? Indeed! thou watchest carefully over thy lord! Do but see where the king's spear is, and the cruse of water that was at his bolster!" And to Saul he said: "Wherefore doth my lord thus pursue after his servant? for what have I done? or what evil is in my hand? Cursed be he that hath thus stirred thee up against me, that I can not abide in the land of the Lord?" Saul again confessed his guilt, and said: "Return, my son David; for I will no more do thee harm, because my soul was precious in thy eyes this day." David answered, and said: "Behold the king's spear! let one of the king's young men come over and fetch it. The Lord may render to every one his righteousness and faithfulness! And thus they again parted with each other.

The hostilities of Saul against David were now drawing to a close. Having been defeated in a battle with the Philistines, the king threw himself on his own sword. In this battle his three sons were also slain. The Philistines took the body of Saul and fastened it to the wall of *Beth-shan*, as a token of their victory. When the inhabitants of *Jabesh-gilead* heard of this outrage, they travelled through a whole night, took the body of Saul at the risk of their lives, carried it to their city for interment, and fasted seven days on account of the death of their king.

On the third day after the battle, a man of the tribe of the Amalekites, came to David, with his clothes rent, and earth upon his head, and informed him of the death of Saul and his sons. "I myself," he added, "have given him the last death-blow in his anguish, and brought thee hither his crown and bracelet." David replied, saying: "How wast thou not afraid to stetch forth thy hand to destroy the Lord's anointed? His blood be upon thy head!" He then commanded one of his young men to

seize and slay him, and wept bitter tears of grief over
Saul and his sons, and expressed his feelings in a most
beautiful hymn of mourning; but he was especially ag-
grieved on account of the loss of his faithful friend Jonathan. "I am distressed," he exclaimed, "for thee, my
brother Jonathan! Very precious hast thou been unto
me: thy love to me was wonderful, passing the love of
all others!"

§ 52. DAVID, KING OF ISRAEL. [2 Samuel ii.-xii.]

After the death of Saul, David and his men went to
Hebron, where he was acknowledged as king by the tribe
of Judah, and reigned seven and a half years. But the
other tribes elected *Ishbosheth*, the son of Saul, king over
themselves. After two years, Ishbosheth was assassinated,
and some time afterwards David became king over the
whole nation. He defeated the neighboring heathen
nations, and extended his empire to the river Euphrates.
He made Jerusalem the capital of the country, and had
the Ark of the Covenant brought there with great exultation, festive processions and solemnities. His piety he
manifested above everything by improving Divine Service.
The sufferings which he had to endure during the years of
his youth, taught him to look up to God and cling to Him.
He began also the erection of a magnificent palace, for
which king *Hiram*, of Tyre, with whom he had made a
treaty of commerce, furnished him with cedar-trees and
carpenters. But being grieved that he should dwell in a
magnificent house of cedar, whereas the Ark of God stood
in a simple tent, he resolved to build a gorgeous temple to
the Lord. But the prophet *Nathan* said to him, in the
name of God: "When thou shalt sleep with thy fathers,
God will give thy kingdom unto thy son, and he shall
build a Temple unto the name of the Lord."

When Abner, one of Saul's captains, was treacherously
murdered, David honored him with a solemn funeral, accompanied him in person to his last resting-place, and punished his murderers. Nor did he forget the covenant of
friendship which he had concluded with Jonathan. As

soon as he had learned that there existed a son of his, he
restored his inheritance to him, and invited him every day
to his table. Both in prosperity and in adversity he looked
up to God, and breathed forth the fervor of his soul in
sacred songs, which we still possess in the *Book of the*
Psalms, that bears his name.

But even once David committed a great sin, and thus
sank deeper as a king than he could ever have sunk as a
simple shepherd. He sent a man to the army, and had a
post assigned to him during battle, where his death was
inevitable, and then took his wife. On account of this
great crime, the prophet Nathan addressed a severe speech
of reproof to him, and, in the name of God, announced to
him lasting misery. The speech of Nathan produced the
deepest pain in the heart of David, which was followed by
his most sincere and fervent repentance. Throughout the
rest of his life he was filled with self-reproach; the joy of
his days and the peace of his soul were gone. Although
God had accorded him forgiveness, yet many a heavy
trouble was the reward of his great sin.

> Wealth and honor cause oft pride,
> Bring dangers manifold;
> Turn the heart from virtue's side,
> Its former strongest hold.

---

§ 53.   THE REBELLION OF ABSALOM.   DEATH OF DAVID.
[2 Samuel xiv.-xix.   1 Kings i. ii.]

The greatest grief which befell David, was caused by
his son *Absalom*. Absalom was a youth of great beauty,
but also of a wicked heart, and continually flattered the
people, stirring up, at the same time, their prejudices
against the just administration of his father. By his
crouching affability, he gained a number of adherents.
He went even so far in his ambition, as to march upon Jerusalem, with the view of robbing his father, both of his
throne and his life. David was compelled to flee, and
" went up by the ascent of mount Olivet, and wept, as he

went up, and had his head covered, and he went barefoot: and all the people that were with him covered every man his head, and they went up weeping, as they ascended the mountain." On his flight from Jerusalem, *Shimei*, of the family of Saul, met him and said to him: "Come out, come out, thou bloody man! thou wicked man! The Lord now revengeth upon thee the blood of Saul, whose throne thou hast usurped; now He has taken the crown from thee, and given it to thy son Absalom! and behold! now thou art in trouble, because thou art a bloody man!" Then said Abishai to the king: "Why should this dead dog curse my lord the king? let me go over, I pray thee, and take off his head." David answered and said: "Let him curse. Behold! mine own son seeketh my life; how much more now may this Benjamite do it! It may be that the Lord will look upon my affliction and requite me good for his cursing this day." David continued on his way, but "Shimei went along on the hill's side over against him, and cursed as he went, and threw stones at him, and cast dust." *Barzillai*, a venerable old man of eighty years, acted differently. He went to meet David, and furnished him and his men with provisions.

David now gathered his men and intended to march in person against his rebellious son; but his faithful followers would not consent to this, and requested him to let them go to battle without him. David yielded, but commanded them, when they marched forth, saying: "Only spare my son Absalom!" The battle was fought, and the men of David defeated his enemies, twenty thousand of whom were slain, while the rest took to flight. Absalom, who rode on a mule, was caught with his long hair in the branches of an oak, so that his mule ran off from under him. A man who saw him in this situation, ran and told *Joab*, who was the chief of David's men, that Absalom was caught in an oak. Joab took three darts in his hand, and thrust them through the heart of Absalom. Then he commanded the trumpets to be blown to retreat, that the people might be spared. Two messengers went, one after the other, to announce to David that his people had gained the victory. The first of them would not, however, inform him of the death of Absalom. When

the second had arrived, David again asked: "Is Absalom
safe?" The messenger replied: May all the enemies of
the king fare like Absalom!" When the king heard
this reply, "he was much moved, and went up to the
chamber over the gate, and wept; and as he went, thus
he said, O my son Absalom, my son, my son Absalom!
would God I had died for thee, O Absalom, my son! my
son!" "And the victory that day was turned into mourning unto the people, for the people heard that day how
the king was grieved for his son."

David returned as king to Jerusalem. and was greeted
by all the people with great rejoicing. Shimei also came
and implored the king's forgiveness, when Abishai said:
"Shall now Shimei be put to death for this because he
cursed the Lord's anointed?" But David said to Shimei:
"Thou shalt not die." Others who had remained faithful
to the king during the revolt, and among these the venerable Barzillai, received the blessing of David, while their
children received other substantial rewards. After some
other calamities, the life of David drew to its close.
When he felt that his end was approaching, he assembled
the elders of Israel at Jerusalem and sa'd to them: "Hear
me, my brethren, and my people: As for me, I had in my
heart to build a house of rest for the ark of the covenant
of the Lord; but God said unto me, Thou shalt not build
a house for my name, because thou hast been a man of
war, and hast shed blood. Solomon, thy son, he shall
build my house and my courts; for I have chosen him to
be my son, and I will be his father. Now, therefore, in
the sight of all Israel, the congregation of the Lord, and
in the audience of our God, keep and seek for all the commandments of the Lord your God: that ye·may possess
this good land, and leave it for an inheritance for your
children after you forever. And thou, Solomon, my son,
know thou the God of thy father, and serve him with a
perfect heart and with a willing mind: for the Lord
searcheth all hearts, and understandeth all the imagina-
tions of the thoughts: if thou seek Him, He will be found
of thee; but if thou forsake him, He will cast thee off
forever." And the princes of Israel offered for the house
of God five thousand talents of gold, ten thousand talents

of silver, eighteen thousand talents of brass, and one hundred thousand talents of iron; and the people rejoiced, for they offered willingly with all their hearts; and David also greatly rejoiced, and praised God, and spoke before the whole congregation, saying: "Thine, O Lord, is the greatness, and the power, and the glory, and the victory, and the majesty: for all that is in the heaven and in the earth is Thine! Thine is the kingdom, O Lord, and Thou art exalted as head above all. Both riches and honor come of Thee, and Thou reignest over all; and in Thy hand is p w r and might; and in thy hand it is to make great, and to give strength unto all. Now, therefore, our God, we thank Thee, and praise Thy glorious name. But who am I, and what is my people, that we should be able to offer so willingly after this sort? for all things come of Thee, and of Thine own have we given Thee. For we are strangers before Thee, and sojourners, as were all our fathers: our days on the earth are as a shadow, and there is none abiding. O Lord our God, all this store that we have prepared to build Thee a house for Thy holy name cometh of Thine hand, and is all Thine own. I know also, my God that Thou triest the heart, and hast pleasure in uprightness. As for me, in the uprightness of my heart I have offered willingly all these things, and I have seen with joy how willingly Thy people have offered unto Thee. O Lord! preserve forever such devotion and such thoughts in the heart of Thy people, and incline their hearts forever unto Thee. And unto my son Solomon give an upright heart, to keep Thy commandments, Thy statutes, to love Thee, and serve Thee forever."

And when the hour had come that he was to die, he caused *Solomon* to be anointed king over Israel, and all the people exclaimed: "God save King Solomon!" Then David called Solomon to his bedside, and said to him: "I go the way of all the earth; be thou therefore strong, and show thyself a man; walk in the ways of the Lord, and keep His commandments, that thou mayest prosper in all that thou doest." Then David fell asleep in the arms of death, and was buried in the "*City of David.*" "And the days that David reigned over Israel were forty years; seven years reigned he in *Hebron*, and thirty and three years reigned he in *Jerusalem.*

---

§ 54.   SOLOMON.   [1 Kings ii.-xi.]

Solomon was the son of David, and disciple of the prophet Nathan—could he be but wise and pious? When he entered upon the government of Israel, he implored God, not for earthly treasures, but for wisdom and understanding, and God not only granted his petition, but gave him also power and riches.

Soon an opportunity presented itself to Solomon to give proof of his wisdom. Two mothers once came to him for his decision in a contest between them. One of them said: "I and this woman slept in one chamber. And it came to pass that the child of this woman died, and she arose at midnight, and took my child from beside me, and laid her dead child in my lap." Now the other replied, saying: "Nay: but the living is my child, and the dead is thy child." When the king heard these words, he said: "Bring me a sword; divide the living child in two, and give half to the one and half to the other." The right mother, having sympathy with her child, at once exclaimed: "O my lord! give her the living child, and in no wise slay it." From these words the king perceived that she was the real mother of the child, and said: "Give her the living child, and in no wise slay it; she is the mother thereof." And all Israel heard of this wise decision, and Solomon's fame spread in distant lands. And there came of all people to see him, and to hear his wisdom. His profound thoughts he exhibited in short sentences and maxims, a great portion of which are still preserved, and form one of the Biblical books.

Solomon acquired also immense riches. He had forty thousand stalls of horses for his chariots, and twelve thousand horsemen. The country enjoyed, during his reign, the blessing of peace, of which he availed himself for the benefit of his people. He entered into treaties with other nations, and these promoted the commerce and prosperity of Israel. Already in the fourth year of his reign, he began the erection of the magnificent temple on Mount *Moriah*, as his father had commanded him. He employed thirty thousand men who cut the timber, seventy thousand porters of burdens, and eighty thousand hewers of stone. All sacred utensils, the altar, the candlesticks, and the door-hinges, were of the purest gold; even the walls were inlaid with gold. After seven years this magnificent edifice was completed. Now Solomon assembled the whole people for the solemn consecration of the temple, and caused the Ark of the Covenant to be carried from Zion into the sanctuary with great pomp and solemnities. He himself stepped before the altar, spread forth his hands toward heaven, and said: "Lord God of Israel! behold the heaven and heaven of heavens cannot contain Thee, how much less this house that I have builded? Yet have thou respect unto the prayer of Thy servant, and to his supplication, O Lord my God, to hearken unto the cry and to the prayer which Thy servant prayeth before Thee to-day: that Thine eyes may be open toward this house night and day, even toward the place of which Thou hast said, ‘My name shall be there:’ that Thou mayest hearken unto the prayer which Thy servant shall make toward this place. And hearken Thou to the supplication of Thy servant, and of Thy people Israel, when they shall pray toward this place: and hear Thou in heaven, Thy dwelling-place: and when Thou hearest, forgive. What prayer and supplication soever be made by any man, or by all Thy people Israel, which shall know every man the plague of his own heart, and spread forth his hands toward this house: then hear Thou in heaven Thy dwelling-place, and forgive, and do, and give to every man according to his ways, whose heart Thou knowest; for Thou, even Thou only, knowest the hearts of all the children of men; that they may fear Thee all the days that they live in the land which Thou gavest unto our fathers. Moreover concerning a *stranger*, that is not of Thy people Israel, but cometh out of a far country for Thy name's sake: when he shall come and pray toward this house; hear Thou in heaven, Thy dwelling-place, and do according to all that the stranger calleth to Thee for; that *all people of the earth* may know Thy name, to fear Thee, as do Thy people Israel; and that they may know that this house, which I have builded, is called by Thy name." Then Solomon stood up, blessed the whole congregation, and said: "Praised be the Lord! the Lord our God be with us, as he was with our fathers!" And the king, together with all Israel, offered sacrifices before the Lord.

Thus the whole house of Israel consecrated the temple of the Lord, "and blessed the king, and went unto their tents, joyful and glad of heart, for all the goodness that the Lord had done for David His servant, and for Israel His people."

Solomon was the happiest of all kings of Israel; his power and dominion increased more and more. But toward the end of his reign, his heart went astray from God, and he did evil in the sight of the Lord. On account of this, God announced to him that his kingdom should not last. This prediction soon began to be fulfilled; the Aramœans of Damascus established their independence, and revolts were attempted even among the Israelites. But he did not live long enough to see the result of these rebellions; he died after a reign of forty years, and the calamity announced to him broke upon his nation soon after his death.

---

§ 55.   THE SEPARATION OF THE KINGDOM.   3010 A.M.
[1 Kings xii.-xiv.]

Solomon having drained the people by heavy taxes, and the nation itself, led astray by the evil example of its king, having given itself up to increasing luxuries, became by degrees too poor, henceforth, to pay the usual taxes. When, therefore, *Rehoboam*, the son of Solomon, had been acknowledged king over Israel, the whole congregation of the people came to him, saying: "Thy father made our yoke grievous; now, therefore, make thou the grievous service of thy father, and his heavy yoke which he put upon us, lighter, and we will serve thee." Rehoboam, desirous to consider the matter, requested them to return after three days for his answer. In the meanwhile he consulted the aged and experienced counsellors of his father, and these advised him to yield to the requests of the people. But his younger and more violent friends advised him to increase the burthens of the nation, and thus to humiliate their presumptuousness. Now, when the people returned on the third day, the king said to them: "My father made your yoke heavy, and I will add to your yoke; my father chastised you with whips, but I will chastise you with scorpions."* Embittered by this haughty reply, ten tribes revolted, and chose a king for themselves, whose name was *Jeroboam*. Only the tribes of Judah and Benjamin, and a portion of the Levites, remained faithful to Rehoboam. The Kingdom of the ten tribes was called the *Kingdom of Israel*, and that of the tribes of Judah and Benjamin, the *Kingdom of Judah*. The kingdom of Israel was governed, in succession, by nineteen kings, who at first resided in *Shechem*, then in *Tirzah*, and at last in *Samaria*. The kingdom of Judah was ruled over, in succession, by twenty kings, all of whom resided in Jerusalem.

The dissolution of the kingdom produced the saddest results, and was one of the greatest calamities that ever befell the people of Israel. One kingdom waged war with the other; one king supplanted another; the worship of God was neglected; the kings and the people sank deeper and deeper into idolatry, vice and ignorance; the prosperity of the country vanished, and foreign princes subjected the people under their rule. God often admonished them to mend their ways; but His admonitions were of little or no avail; and the nation thus hastened toward its destruction.

* Scorpions are whips armed with pointed thorns, or intertwisted with iron wires, to produce severe wounds by their blows.

C. The Kings of Israel.

§ 56. JEROBOAM.

Jeroboam, as we have just learned, was elected king of Israel, and made Shechem the seat of his government. Already, during the reign of king Solomon, the prophet Ahiah had foretold him that he should become king, and his house continue to reign, if he would walk in the ways of the Lord. But Jeroboam soon went astray. His chief object was to secure his government, to build strong cities, and employ all possible means to maintain himself in opposition to Rehoboam. He introduced idolatry into Israel, erected two golden calves, one at Bethel, and the other at Dan, and caused divine adoration to be paid to them, fearing the people might return to the rule of Rehoboam, if it continued to go to the temple of Jerusalem. He either performed himself the priestly functions, or selected the priests from classes of the people that were not of the tribe of Levi, and changed even, in a most high-handed manner, the days of the Festivals. The people, either from ignorance or the desire of comfort and repose, made no objection to these sacrilegious inroads into their inherited religion. But God, in His mercy, sent a prophet to admonish the king, and, at the same time, announce to him that a descendant of David should destroy his idols. But Jeroboam did not repent or mend his ways. All at once his son was taken sick, and, as the king had no confidence in his own idols, he sent his wife in disguise to the *Jewish* prophet Ahiah, to learn the final fate of his child. The prophet informed her that, before she should have passed the threshold of her house, her child would be dead; and that her whole race should be blotted out, because Jeroboam had not listened to God's admonitions. This announcement was fulfilled. Jeroboam died after a reign of twenty-two years, and was succeeded by his son Nadab.

§ 57. The Kings of Israel. (*Continued.*)

NADAB—BAASHA—ELAH—ZIMRI—OMRI—AHAB.

Nadab, the son of Jeroboam, was slain, together with his whole family, after a reign of two years, by *Baasha*, who then ascended the throne of Israel. Baasha continued the hostilities which Jeroboam had commenced against the kingdom of Judah, removed his seat of government to Tirzah, carried on a war against Asa, king of Judah, with ill luck, led a wicked life, and died after a reign of twenty-four years. He was succeeded by his son *Elah*, who after reigning only two years, was assassinated by *Zimri*, one of his captains, who immediately proclaimed himself king, and slew the whole family of Elah. But Zimri reigned only seven days; for an army of Israelites, that was engaged in the siege of *Gibbethon*, a city of the Philistines, having heard of his conspiracy, proclaimed their leader, *Omri*, king of Israel. When Zimri heard this and found that he was without all hope of escape, he retired to his palace, set it on fire, and perished in the flames.

The people were now divided into two parties; but the party of Omri maintained the ascendancy, and he was proclaimed king by the people also.

He removed the seat of government to *Samaria*, and "wrought evil in the sight of the Lord, and did worse than all that were before him." He reigned twelve years, and was succeeded by his son *Ahab*, one of the most wicked kings that ever ruled over Israel. His reign lasted twenty-two years—a long period under such an impious king! Sin and destruction, nurtured for such a long time, could take firm root. He was not content with following the example of Jeroboam, to renew the worship of calves and idols, and build·altars and temples to false gods, but married also *Jezebel*, the daughter of the Sidonian prince *Ethbaal*, and practised, with the view of pleasing and honoring her, the idolatry of her people, the worship of Baal, in the most solemn manner, even at the seat of the government. Idolatry now became the religion of the land, and the difference between Israelites and heathens thus vanished from the country. And since that time, false worship never ceased in the kingdom of Israel. The prophets of the Lord were slain, and their place given to four hundred prophets of Baal, and four hundred prophets of the Worship of the Groves. Such wickedness had thitherto not been committed in Israel.

In the days of Ahab, there lived a prophet in Gilead, named *Elijah*, with the surname of *Tishbi*. He suddenly came forth from his solitude, stepped before Ahab, and said to him in the name of God: "As the Lord God of Israel liveth, before whom I stand, there shall not be dew nor rain during these years, unless I command it."

This prophecy was soon followed by its fulfillment. A long drought caused a fearful famine, want and misery in Israel; the fields lay parched, and men and animals longed for refreshing waters; Elijah, however at the command of God, was fed by ravens, in his concealment near the Brook Cherith. But this brook also dried up after some time, and God said to Elijah: "Arise, get thee to Zarephath; there a widow shall sustain thee." Elijah obeyed; and when he came to the gate of the city, he met the widow just engaged in gathering wood; he said to her: "Fetch me, I pray thee, a little water, that I may drink, and a morsel of bread to eat." The widow replied, saying: "As the Lord liveth, I have no bread, but only a handful of meal and a little oil; and behold, I am now gathering a little wood, that I may prepare a repast for myself and my son, alas! perhaps the last we shall have on earth!" And Elijah said to her: "Fear not; the Lord shall not suffer thee to be in want—do as I have requested thee." The good widow went and gave the prophet the only food left in her house, and God afterwards provided her with all necessary means for her subsistence. Her son, also, who was in a dying state, rose again upon the prayer of Elijah. and fully regained his health.

§ 58. Elijah and Ahab.

The famine and misery increased more and more in the land, so that the king himself was compelled to travel about to seek food and water for his horses. At last, God had again mercy upon His people, and said to Elijah: "Go and show thyself to Ahab; for now I will again send rain upon the earth." When Ahab and Elijah met, the latter said to the prophet: "Art thou he that troubleth Israel?" Elijah replied, saying: "Not I have troubled Israel; but thou and thy father's house, in that ye have forsaken the commandments of the Lord, and thou hast followed the idols of Baal. Now, therefore, send and gather to me all Israel unto Mount *Carmel*, and the prophets of Baal four hundred and fifty, and the prophets of the groves four hundred, that eat at Jezebel's table."

When Ahab had complied with this command. Elijah stepped before the assembly of the people, and addressed them thus: "How long halt ye between two opinions? if the Lord be God, follow him: but if Baal, then follow him." And the people answered him not a word. Then said Elijah unto the people: "I, even I only, remain a prophet of the Lord; but Baal's prophets are four hundred and fifty men. Let them therefore give us two bullocks; and let them choose one bullock for themselves, and cut it in pieces, and lay it on wood, and put no fire under; and I will dress the other bullock, and lay it on wood, and put no fire under: and call ye on the name of your gods, and I will call on the name of the Lord; and the God that answereth by fire, let him be God." And all the people answered and said: "It is well spoken." And Elijah said unto the prophets of Baal: "Choose you one bullock for yourselves, and dress it first; for ye are many: and call on the name of your gods, but put no fire under." And they took the bullock which was given them, and they dressed it, and called on the name of Baal from morning even until noon, saying: "O Baal, hear us." But there was no voice, nor any that answered. And they leaped upon the altar that was made. And it came to pass at noon, that Elijah mocked them, and said: "Cry aloud: for he is a god; either he is talking, or he is pursuing, or he is in a journey, or peradventure he sleepeth, and must be awakened." And they cried aloud, and cut themselves after their manner with knives and lancets, till the blood gushed out upon them.

Elijah then built an altar, made a trench around it, arranged the wood, cut the bullock in pieces, and laid him upon the wood. When the time of the evening sacrifice had come, the prophet prostrated himself to the earth, and prayed thus: "Lord God of Abraham, Isaac, and of Israel, let it be known this day that Thou art God in Israel, and that I am Thy servant, and that I have done all these things at Thy word. Hear me, O Lord, hear me, that this people may know that Thou art the Lord God, and that Thou hast turned their hearts back again." This was but a short prayer, but it came from the depth of the prophet's heart, and God hearkened to it: lightening descended from heaven, and consumed the burnt-sacrifice. And the people, seeing all this with their own eyes, fell upon their faces, and exclaimed with one voice: "*The Lord alone is God! The Lord alone is God!*" But Elijah said to them: "Take the prophets of Baal!" The people fulfilled this command, and put them to death at the brook *Kishon.* And the heavens grew black with thick clouds—abundant rain poured down, and refreshed the soil, so that shortly afterwards there was again plenty of food in the land of Israel.

This event caused the people to improve; but Ahab continued in his wonted wickedness; he still remained the blind tool of his impious wife, as may be seen from the following occurrence: *Naboth*, the Jezreelite, had a vineyard hard by the king's palace. Ahab desired to possess this vineyard, but Naboth would not part with it, because it was an inheritance of his fathers. This refusal filled the king with displeasure and sorrow, that he could neither eat nor drink. But his wife soon found means to gratify the desire of her royal consort. She hired false witnesses who accused Naboth of treason and blasphemy. The poor Naboth was found guilty, and stoned to death; whereupon Ahab quietly took possession of the vineyard. Now Elijah stepped before him, and said: "Hast thou killed, and also taken possession? Behold! in the place where dogs licked the blood of Naboth, there dogs shall lick thy blood, even thine; and dogs shall eat Jezebel by the wall of Jezreel."

Shortly afterwards, Ahab. declared war to the Syrians, although a prophet of the Lord had announced to him that he should not return alive. And so it happened. A man drew his bow, as by chance, and his arrow hit the king in the heart; wherefore he said to the driver of his chariot: "Turn thy hand, and carry me out of the host; for I am wounded." The driver of the king's chariot did as his master had commanded. Towards evening Ahab was dead. As the blood from his wounds had soiled his chariot, it was washed in the pool of Samaria, and dogs licked it up, as the prophet had predicted. Such are God's judgments!

§ 59. Ahaziah—Jehoram—Jehu—Jezebel's Death.

Ahab was succeeded by his son *Ahaziah*, who led an impious life, like his parents. He reigned only two years, and died in consequence of a fall through a lattice in his upper chamber. He was succeeded by his brother *Jehoram*, who did evil in the eyes of God, but carried his wickedness not so far as his father Ahab. One day a disciple of the prophets came to *Ramoth* and said to *Jehu*, one of the Israelitish captains: "I have come to anoint thee king over the people of the Lord, over Israel. And thou shalt smite the house of Ahab thy master, that I may avenge the blood of my servants, the prophets, and the blood of all the servants of the Lord, at the hand of Jezebel." Jehu at once marched toward Jezreel, where Jehoram, and *Ahaziah*, king of Judah, just then sojourned. When Jehoram learned from the watchman on the tower that an army was approaching, he went with Ahaziah to meet Jehu, with a view of inducing him to peace and friendship. They met in the vineyard of Naboth, and Jehoram asked Jehu: "Is it peace?" The latter replied: "What! peace, so long as the outrages of thy mother Jezebel and her witchcrafts are so many?" When Jehoram heard these words he attempted to fly: but Jehu drew a bow with his full strength, and shot an arrow through his heart Then he said to his captain *Bidkar*: "Take him up, and cast him into the field of Naboth; for I remember what the Lord hath said, 'I will avenge the blood of Naboth in this field.'" Thus Ahab's blood flowing forth from the veins of his son, was shed, according to the divine announcement, upon the same ground which had drunk the innocent blood of Naboth. When *Ahaziah* saw the gloomy death of Jehoram, he attempted to fly, but Jehu pursued him, and caused him also to be slain.

Jehu then continued his way toward Jezreel. When Jezebel heard of his approach, she painted her face, ornamented her head, looked out from the window of the palace, and said to Jehu: "Had Zimri peace, who slew his master?" Jehu lifted up his eyes to the window, and said to the chamberlains that stood by her: "Throw her down!" They immediately obeyed this command, and her blood was sprinkled upon the wall, and her body trampled by the hoofs of the horses in the street. When Jehu, after some hours, ordered her burial, no more of her was found than her skull, her feet, and her hands; for dogs had eaten up the rest. Thus the words of the prophet were fulfilled.

---

§ 60.   THE PROPHET ELISHA.   [2 Kings ii.-vi.]

One of the most faithful disciples of Elijah was *Elisha*. God himself commanded Elijah to anoint him to be prophet in his stead, which he did, when he met him as he was ploughing the field of his father, by throwing his mantle upon him. By this symbolical act he meant to say: "Be what I am, a prophet of God, and follow me!" Elisha, at once understood the symbol, left his oxen, and said to Elijah: "Let me, I pray thee, kiss my father and my mother, and then I will follow thee." This request being granted, Elisha did as he had asked, and thenceforth accompanied his master everywhere, and became a most zealous servant of God. When Elijah felt that his end was approaching, he said to Elisha: "Ask what I shall do for thee, before I be taken away from thee."

Elisha answered: "I pray thee, let a double portion of thy spirit be upon me." His later acts proved that God fulfilled this noble wish. How he delighted to do good and help the suffering, may be seen from the following narrative.

Naaman, the general of the Syrian king, was stricken with leprosy. An Israelitish maiden, who waited on Naaman's wife, said to her mistress: "Would God my Lord were with the prophet Elisha! for he would cure him of his leprosy." Naaman at once acted upon this wish, and went with his horses and his chariot and many presents to the prophet. Elisha sent a messenger to him, saying: "Go and wash in Jordan seven times, and thou shalt be clean." But Naaman got angry at this speech, and said: "Behold, I thought he would surely come out to me, and call on the name of the Lord his God, and move his hand over the place, and thus cure me of my disease." His servants endeavored to pacify him, and said: "If the prophet had bid thee do some great thing, wouldst thou not have done it? How much rather, then, when he saith to thee, 'Wash and be clean?'" These words produced a proper effect. Naaman descended from his chariot, dipped himself seven times in Jordan, and behold! he rose from the water entirely clean from leprosy. Full of joy, he at once returned to Elisha, and said: "*Behold, now I know that there is no God in all the earth like the God of Israel!*" He then offered him precious gifts as a reward for his cure; but the prophet refused to accept them, well satisfied with this, that he had made him a worshipper of his God.

But *Gehazi*, the prophet's servant, did not entertain the same noble thoughts. When Naaman had left the house, he ran after him and asked of him, in the name of his master, one talent, and two changes of garments. Naaman most joyfully gave him even more than he had asked. When Elisha, who had not sent his servant, heard of this fraud, he got very angry, and severely reproved him for his shameful conduct. Nor did God let Gehazi go unpunished for his fraud and extortion; the leprosy of Naaman came over him, so that he was all over his body as white as snow.

One day, when Elisha was going towards the town of Beth-el, some rude boys came from the city and mocked him, saying: "Go up, thou bald head! go up, thou bald head!" The prophet looked at them, and told them that it could not be well with such ill-bred and mischievous children. And his words were soon fulfilled. No sooner had he concluded his speech, than two bears came forth from the woods, and tore forty-two of them in pieces.

Elisha filled the office of prophet for more than fifty years after the death of Elijah, under the reign of the kings *Jehoram, Jehu, Jehoahaz, and Jehoash.* When the aged prophet lay upon his death-bed, king Jehoash paid him a visit, wept, and exclaimed: "O my father, my father, the chariot of Israel and the horses thereof!"

§ 61. The Prophet Jonah.

At the time of *Jeroboam II.*, king of Israel, who was the son of Jehoash, there lived *Jonah*, whom the Lord had appointed not only prophet for Israel, but also for the heathens. He sent him to Nineveh, the capital of Assyria, which was from fifty to sixty miles long, "to cry against it, because their wickedness had come up before Him." But Jonah, instead of obeying the divine command, went on board a ship to go to *Tarshish*, and thus to flee from God. But God stirred up a fierce tempest, a mighty thunderstorm arose, and the ship was near being foundered. The sailors became greatly alarmed, and every one of them prayed to his God. But Jonah being unable to pray, because his conscience naturally troubled him on account of his evil deed, went down into the hollow of the ship and fell asleep. Then the ship-master went to him, and said: "What meanest thou, O sleeper? Arise, call upon thy God? Perhaps *thy* God will think upon us, that we perish not.

Then the superstitious heathen mariners said to one another: "Come, and let us cast lots, that we may know for whose cause this evil is upon us." The lot fell upon Jonah. Yet the mariners, though they were but heathens, had pity upon him, and hesitated to deliver him up to the stormy waves. Once more they attempted to bring their ship to the shore: but seeing that all their exertions were in vain, they cast him into the sea; and behold! the sea immediately ceased to rage. But by God's wonderful ordination, Jonah was delivered from the waves, and he reached the land in safety. And now he hastened to Nineveh and cried aloud: "Yet forty days, and Nineveh shall be overthrown!"

This proclamation of the prophet produced the most salutary effect; all the inhabitants of the city, from the greatest even to the least of them, repented and turned from their evil ways; the king himself arose from his throne, laid off his royal robe, covered himself with sackcloth, sat in ashes, and caused the following proclamation to me made in Nineveh: "Let neither man nor beast, herd nor flock, taste any thing: let them not feed, nor drink water: But let men and beast be covered with sackcloth, and cry mightily unto God: yea, let them turn every one from his evil way, and from the violence that is in their hands. Who can tell if God will turn and repent, and turn away from His fierce anger, that we perish not?" The people obeyed the exhortation of their worthy king, and repented: and the Lord, seeing that they had turned from their evil ways, did not send the threatened calamities, but spared the city. Jonah grew indignant at the compassion thus shown to Nineveh, and prayed: "I pray Thee, O Lord, was not this my saying, when I was yet in my country? Therefore I fled before unto Tarshish: for I knew that Thou art a gracious God, and merciful, slow to anger, and of great kindness, and repentest Thee of the evil. Therefore now, O Lord, take, I beseech Thee, my life from me; for it is better for me to die than to live." But the Lord reproved him in a most indulgent manner. Jonah having seated himself outside of the city, to see what would become of it, God caused a gourd to grow, which afforded him refreshing shade, and protection from the burning rays of the sun. The prophet exceedingly rejoiced at this gourd. But God sent, on the next morning, a worm, which destroyed the gourd; and the sun beat so severely on the head of Jonah, that he grew faint, and again wished to die. Then said God to him: "Doest

thou well to be angry for the gourd? Thou hast had pity
on the gourd, for the which thou hast not labored, neither
madest it grow: which came up in a night and perished
in a night: And should I not spare Nineveh, that great
city, wherein are more than six-score thousand persons
that can not discern between their right hand and their
left hand; and also much cattle?"

§ 62. Job.

Other instances also are found in the ancient world,
which show that strong virtuous sentiments, and fear of
God, sometimes lived in the hearts of non-Israelites. Thus
Holy writ relates that there dwelt once in the land of *Uz*
a very rich and pious man, named JOB. He had seven
sons and three daughters, seven thousand sheep, three
thousand camels, five hundred yoke of oxen, five hundred
she-asses, and a very numerous household. Being a very
pious man, with all his wealth, he enjoyed the greatest
happiness. But God, wishing to try him, whether he
would remain constant in adversity, visited him with
heavy afflictions. His children, his cattle, and all else that
he possessed, perished. Yet, he did not murmur, but exclaimed: "*The Lord gave, the Lord hath taken away,
blessed be the name of the Lord!*" He himself was taken
sick, and became so leprous, that he sat upon a dung-hill
and took a potsherd to scrape the sores from his body.
Still he remained pious and God-fearing. Then said his
wife to him: "Dost thou still retain thine integrity?" to
which Job answered: "Thou speakest as one of the foolish women speaketh. What! shall we receive good at
the hand of God, and shall we not receive evil also?"
And he still persevered in his trust in God.

Three of his friends, *Eliphaz, Bildad*, and *Zopha*, heard
of the affliction which had befallen him, and agreed to visit
and console him in his sufferings. When they raised their
eyes afar off, and could hardly recognize their friend, they
wept, sat down with him upon the ground seven days and
seven nights, and did not speak to him; for they saw that

his grief was very great. After this, Job opened his mouth and complained of his excessive sufferings: yet, the innocence and purity of his own conscience, and his confidence in God's justice, afforded him consolation. But his friends thought that his sufferings had been caused by some guilt of his, since God never inflicted woe upon man, unless he deserved it in consequence of his sin. Such speeches grieved the unhappy Job very much; his inward pain increased, and he cursed the day on which he was born. But soon the piety of his heart, and his love for God, awoke again, and he consoled himself with the reflection: "I know that my God liveth, who will awaken me from death unto everlasting life."

By his patience and constancy, he regained the grace and favor of God. The Lord restored to him all that he had lost, and even redoubled his former wealth. His relatives and friends visited him again, ate with him, and sympathized with him.

After this, Job lived yet one hundred and forty years, saw his sons, his sons' sons, even to the fourth generation, and died, very old and full of days.

----

§ 63. The Destruction of the Kingdom of Israel.— The Prophets. [2 Kings xvii.] 3268 A.M.

While the *only* exhortation to repentance addressed by the prophet Jonah to the heathen inhabitants of Nineveh, produced the desired effect, the Israelites remained unmoved by a hundred similar admonitions. They heaped sin upon sin, misdeed upon misdeed! All the successors of Ahab were wicked, and misled the people to idolatry and vice. For this reason God sent several prophets to admonish them to repent, to announce His judgments, and at the same time, proclaim His mercy, if they would return from their evil ways.

Hosea arose, announced the approaching destruction of the kingdom, and the captivity of its inhabitants, if they

would not repent. "Hear the word of the Lord," he ex
claimed, "ye children of Israel! Ye swear, and steal, and
murder, and commit violence, and heap crime upon crime.
But the time of judgment shall come, when the Lord will
reject you, and disperse you among the nations." On the
other hand, Hosea promised them also the loving forgiveness of the Lord, if they would repent and return to Him.

Amos, who was a shepherd at Tekoa, and afterwards
became a prophet, proclaimed his prophecies at Beth-el,
where the Israelites worshipped calves. Although he had
not been trained in the schools of prophets, yet he understood it well, to expose in soul-stirring speeches, even
in the face of kings, the atrocious deeds of Israel. "Hear,
ye lords of Samaria," he exclaimed, "who oppress the
poor, who crush the needy, who say to their masters,
Bring, and let us drink. The Lord hath sworn by His
holiness, that, behold! the days shall come upon you, that
He will take you away with hooks, and your posterity
with fish-hooks. I will send you into captivity, and I will
sift the house of Israel among all nations, as the corn is
sifted in a sieve, yet shall not the least grain fall upon the
earth. All the sinners of my people shall die by the sword,
who say, 'The evil shall not overtake us.' I have smitten
you with blasting and mildew; I have caused your fig-
trees and your olive-trees to be devoured by the palmer-
worm: yet ye have not returned unto me, saith the Lord.
I have sent among you the pestilence; your young men
have I slain with the sword, and have taken away your
horses; yet have ye not returned unto me, saith the Lord.
I have caused destruction among you, as once in Sodom
and Gomorrah, and ye were as a firebrand plucked out of
the flames, yet have ye not returned unto me, saith the
Lord: therefore will I do thus unto thee."

The prophet *Micah* likewise describes with bold open-
ness, the vices both of the high and the low of the house
of Judah as well as of the house of Israel. "Woe to
them," he exclaims, "that devise iniquity, and work evil
upon their beds! when the morning is light, they practise
it because it is in the power of their hand. And they
covet fields and take them by violence: and houses, and

take them away; therefore punishment is not afar off."
"Hear, this, ye heads of the house of Jacob, and princes
of the house of Israel, who build up Zion with blood, and
Jerusalem with iniquity, for your sake shall Zion be
ploughed as a field, and Jerusalem shall become a heap of
ruins, and the mountain of the Temple as the high places
of the forest." The prophet then reproved his people for
this, that they clung more to outward worship than to the
observance of the moral law, and assured them that they
could easily regain the mercy of God, if they would but
return from their evil ways. "The Lord," he exclaims,
"hath showed thee, O man, what is good : and what else
doth the Lord require of thee, but to practise justice, to
love charity, and to walk humbly with thy God?"

The prophet *Joel* pronounced the following proclamation: "Hear this, Israel! the day of the Lord is at hand,
the day of destruction, whereof ye shall tell your children
and your children's children. That which the palmer-worm
hath left shall be eaten by the locust—and that which the
locusts will leave, shall be eaten by the canker-worm;
and that which the canker-worm will leave, shall be eaten
by the cater-pillar. Their teeth shall be as the teeth of a
lion. The field shall be wasted, the land shall mourn;
the husbandmen shall wail, the winedressers shall howl.
the beasts of the field shall groan; the rivers shall be
dried up, and the fire shall devour the pastures of the wilderness. Therefore, if ye turn to the Lord, with all your
heart, and with fasting and with weeping, and with mourning, ye shall know that God is in the midst of Israel.

The prophet *Isaiah* also exposed their misdeeds, and
admonished them to repent, saying: hear, O heavens,
and give ear, O earth : for the Lord hath spoken, I have
nourished and brought up children, and they have rebelled
against me. The ox knoweth his owner, and the ass his
master's crib: but Israel doth not know, my people doth
not consider. Ah sinful nation, a people laden with iniquity, a seed of evildoers, children that are corrupters :
they have forsaken the Lord, they have provoked the
Holy One of Israel unto anger, they are gone away back-

ward. Hear the word of the Lord, ye rulers of Sodom;
give ear unto the law of our God, ye people of Gomorrah.
To what purpose is the multitude of your sacrifices unto
me? saith the Lord: I am full of the burnt offerings of
rams, and the fat of fed beasts; and I delight not in the
blood of bullocks, or of lambs, or of he-goats. When ye
come to appear before me, who hath required this at your
hand, to tread my courts? Bring no more vain oblations;
incense is an abomination unto me: the new moons and
sabbaths, the calling of assemblies, I can not away with;
it is iniquity, even the solemn meeting. Your new moons
and your appointed feasts my soul hateth: they are a
trouble unto me; I am weary to bear them. And when
ye spread forth your hands, I will hide mine eyes from
you; yea, when ye make many prayers, I will not hear:
your hands are full of blood. Wash you, make you clean;
put away the evil of your doings from before mine eyes,
cease to do evil; learn to do well; seek judgment, relieve
the oppressed, judge the fatherless, plead for the widow.
Come now, and let us reason together saith the Lord:
though your sins be as scarlet, they shall be as white as
snow; though they be red like crimson, they shall be as
wool. If ye be willing and obedient, ye shall eat the good
of the land; but if ye refuse and rebel, ye shall be devoured
with the sword: for the mouth of the Lord hath spoken it."

The prophet *Nahum* said: "God is jealous, and a re-
venger, the Lord is slow in anger, and great in power,
and will not at all acquit the wicked; He hath His way
in the whirlwind, and in the storm, and the clouds are the
dust of His feet. He rebuketh the sea, and maketh it
dry, and drieth up all the rivers. The mountains quake
at Him, and the hills melt, the earth trembleth before His
countenance, and its inhabitants. Who can stand before
His indignation?"

The prophet *Habakkuk* said: "Thus saith the Lord, I
will work a work in your days, which ye will not believe,
though it be told you. For, lo, I raise up the Chaldeans,
that bitter and hasty nation, and they shall gather captives
as the sand."

Zephaniah said: "Woe to the rebellious and oppressing city! She obeys not the voice, she trusteth not in the Lord—she draws not nigh to her God. Therefore, I shall gather nations, that I may assemble the kingdoms, to pour upon them mine indignation, even all my fierce anger. But I will also judge all that afflict thee, and I will save the oppressed, and gather them that were driven out, and I will make you a name and a praise among all the nations of the earth."

Such and many other similar exhortations were addressed by the prophets to the Israelites. But all in vain; they would not heed the warning voice of those faithful servants of the Lord. At last, God's mercy and long-suffering, so long exercised over them, were exhausted, and His infallible judgment hastened toward its fulfillment. He chose *Shalmaneser*, king of Assyria, to accomplish the work of judgment. Shalmaneser declared war to *Hoshea*, king of Israel, because he had entered into an alliance with *So*, king of Egypt. After a siege of three years, the city of Samaria was taken and burned down, and the king and his people were carried as captives to Assyria and Media, to settle in uncultivated regions of these countries. On the other hand, Shalmaneser sent inhabitants of Babylon and other countries of his empire, to Samaria and the neighboring places, and with them a Jewish priest, that he might instruct these heathens in the worship of God. While they learned to fear and serve God, they, at the same time continued to practice idolatry. This new population of Samaria became known afterwards as the Sect of the *Samaritans*.

D. The Kings of Judah.

§ 64.   REHOBOAM — ABIJAH — ASA — JEHOSHAPHAT— JEHORAM.

[1 Kings xiv.-xv.   2 Kings viii.   2 Chro. xx.-xxi.]

As the greater number of the kings of Judah were better and more pious than those of Israel, this kingdom lasted one hundred and thirty-four years longer than that of the latter. Many of the kings of Judah also forsook their God, and set their people an evil example. *Rehoboam* the son of Solomon, under whose reign the empire was divided, did much evil in the eyes of the Lord. He was already forty-one years old when he ascended the royal throne, so that it was to be expected that the earnestness and discretion of manhood should guard him against many a rash and wicked deed. But this expectation was not fulfilled. He built high places, and erected statues for idols upon all places, and under every green tree; besides, he suffered corrupted young men to practise all the abominations of the heathens. In punishment for all these iniquities, God sent misery upon him. The Egyptian King *Shishak* marched against Jerusalem, and took away both the treasures of the Temple and the royal house. Now the prophet *Shemaiah* stepped before King Rehoboam and addressed him, saying; "Thus saith the Lord, 'Ye have forsaken me, and therefore have I also left you in the hand of Shishak.'" The princes and the king humbled themselves, and exclaimed: "The Lord is just!" Whereupon God said: "They have humbled themselves, therefore I will not destroy them. Nevertheless, they shall remain subject to Shishak, that they may learn the difference between my service and the service of the kings of strange countries." However merciful this lesson, taught them by God himself, was, it did not produce the desired effect. Rehoboam continued the war with Jeroboam, king of Israel, and died after a reign of seventeen years, leaving his son Abijam as his successor.

Abijam followed the evil example of his father, and made war against the kingdom of Israel, but died after the short reign of but three years.

His son and successor *Asa* was a pious, God-fearing prince; he destroyed all the temples of the idols, and removed their images and statues. His continual wars with Baasha, King of Israel, compelled him to enter into an alliance with the Syrian king, *Benhadad*, in consequence of which the hostilities between the two kings were ended. He died after a reign of forty-one years, and was succeeded by his son.

Jehoshaphat, a pious man and excellent prince. He provided the strong places of the land with garrisons, appointed able officers, and endeavored to gain the respect of the neighboring nations for his own country. But his special care was devoted to the diffusion of the true knowledge of God He destroyed the temples and groves of the idols, and appointed Levites and priests to travel throughout the country with copies of the law, that they might teach the people. "Thus shall ye do," he said to them, "in the fear of the Lord, faithfully, and with a perfect heart; what cause soever shall come to you of your brethren that dwell in their cities, between blood and blood, in their doubts concerning laws and commandments, statutes and judgments, ye shall warn them that they trespass not against the Lord, and the wrath of the Lord come not upon you and upon your brethren." And to the judges he said: "Take heed what you do; for ye judge not for man, but for the Lord, who is with you in the judgment. Wherefore now let the fear of the Lord be upon you, and reflect well, that there is no iniquity with the Lord our God, nor respect of persons, nor taking of bribery."

When shortly afterwards, the Moabites and Ammonites waged war against Judah, Jehoshaphat assembled the people in the Temple of God, and offered up the following prayer: "O Lord God of our fathers, art not thou God in heaven? and rulest not Thou over all the kingdoms of the heathen? and in Thine hand is there not power and might, so that none is able to withstand Thee? Art not Thou our God, who didst drive out the inhabitants of this land before Thy people Israel, and gavest it to the seed of Abraham Thy friend forever? And now, behold, the children of Ammon and Moab and mount Seir, whom Thou wouldst not let Israel invade, when they came out of the Land of Egypt, but they turned from them, and destroyed them not; behold, I say, how they reward us, to come to cast us out of Thy possession, which Thou hast given us to inherit. O our God, wilt Thou not judge them? for we have no might against this great company that cometh against us; neither know we what to do: but our eyes are upon Thee." When he had concluded this prayer,

a God-inspired man rose in the assembly and said:
"Hearken ye, all Judah, and ye inhabitants of Jerusalem
and thou king Jehoshaphat; Thus saith the Lord unto
you, 'Be not afraid nor dismayed by reason of this great
multitude; for the battle is not yours, but God's. To-
morrow go ye down against them; ye shall not need to
fight! Be ye firm, stand ye still, and see the salvation of
the Lord with you. The Eternal will be with you!'"
And the Lord was indeed with them. The enemies were
suddenly seized with fury, fought against. and destroyed
each other, so that the Israelites made such a vast spoil of
precious jewels and vessels, that they were unable to carry
them all away, although they gathered them during three
days. The people then returned with psalteries and trumpets to Jerusalem, and offered their thanks to God in the
Temple. After this delivery, the land enjoyed peace for
twenty-five years. Jehoshaphat reigned twenty-five years.

Jehoram, who succeeded his father, was unlike him.
His wife, *Athaliah*, a daughter of Ahab, misled him to
many evil deeds. He murdered his brothers and many
princes of his kingdom. But the punishment of God soon
came upon him. The Edomites revolted, and the Philistines and Arabians invaded his country, plundered his
palace, and carried away his wives and children. He was
soon visited by a loathsome disease, with which he died.

---

§ 65. The Kings of Judah. (Continued.) Ahaziah—
Jehoash—Amaziah—Uzziah—Jotham—Ahaz—Hezekiah. [2 Kings, xi.-xii. xviii.-xx.]

Jehoram was succeeded by *Ahaziah*, who reigned only
one year, when he was slain, together with Jehoram, king
of Israel. After Ahaziah's death, *Athaliah*, his mother,
usurped the royal throne, and slew all the children of the
king, with the exception of *Jehoash*, whom *Jehosheba*, his
father's sister, concealed for six years in the Temple, and

thus saved him from the persecutions of Athaliah. When Jehoash was seven years old. *Jehoida.* the high priest, stirred up a rebellion against Athaliah, which resulted in her death, and brought Jehoash upon the royal throne. As long as Jehoiada lived and assisted the young king with his counsel, both the people and their ruler fared well, and served their God. The temples of Baal and the idolatrous altars were torn down, and the worship of God re-instated according to its prescribed order and arrangement. After the death of Jehoiadah, Jehoash forsook God and committed great crimes. But his wickedness was soon punished; he was defeated in a war with the Syrians, and had to purchase a dishonorable peace at the price of all his treasures. Soon afterwards, he was murdered in his bed by his own servants.

Jehoash was succeeded by his son *Amaziah*, who caused the murderers of his father to be punished, and fought victoriously against the Edomites. In his war against Jehoash, king of Israel, he was defeated, whereupon Jerusalem was taken and plundered, and all the treasures carried away to Samaria. After a reign of twenty-nine years, a conspiracy was formed against him, which compelled him to flee from Jerusalem. He was overtaken at *Lachish*, and murdered.

His son and successor, *Uzziah*, was a pious prince. He restored the worship of the true God, and devoted his care and attention to the improvement of the affairs of his country, and succeeded in defeating the Philistines, the Arabians and other neighboring tribes. But his power and prosperity led him astray—he usurped the office of priest, for which impious act he was punished with leprosy, which rendered him unable to attend to the duties of his royal dignity, so that he was compelled to associate his son Jotham with him in the government. He died after a reign of fifty-two years, and left his son

Jotham on the royal throne. This king proved a wise, pious, God-fearing, and, therefore, prosperous prince. He defeated the Ammonites, and forced them to pay him a large tribute.   He reigned sixteen years, and was succeeded by his son

Ahaz, who vied with the kings of Israel in atrocities and idolatrous excesses, and went even so far as to erect, in the valley of *Hinnom,* a statue to the Phenician god, *Moloch,* to which infants were offered as sacrifices. Under his reign, the country was invaded by *Rezia,* King of Syria, and *Pekah,* King of Israel. He called *Tiglathpileser,* King of Assyria, to his aid, and was thus made tributary to him. Happily for his country, he died after a reign of but sixteen years.

Under his son and successor, *Hezekiah,* Judah again enjoyed better times of peace and tranquillity. Hezekiah was found just in the eyes of God ; no Jewish king, ever since the time of David, was so filled with God-fearing piety as he. "He removed the high-places, and brake the statues of the idols, and cut down the groves, and brake in pieces the brazen serpent that Moses had made, for unto those days the children of Israel did burn incense to it." Immediately after his accession to the royal throne, he re-opened the Temple of the Lord, had it cleansed, and ordered the celebration of the Passover Feast, to which he invited the whole people, and which was solemnized with Solomonian magnificence and splendor.

In the sixth year of his reign, *Shalmaneser,* king of Assyria, destroyed the kingdom of *Israel,* whereupon *Sennacherib,* his son and successor, conquered all the forti-fied cities of Judah, and then sent his general, *Rabshakeh,* to attack also Jerusalem. Hezekiah sent word to Sen-nacherib, saying : "March away from my land and I will pay all the tribute that thou puttest on me." Sennacherib made great demands, so that Hezekiah was compelled to deliver up to him all the treasure of the Temple and his own house to satisfy him. But notwithstanding all this, Sennacherib soon sent an enormous army against Jerusa-lem, and demanded the complete subjection of Hezekiah. Rabshakeh. Sennacherib's general, sent word to the Jews, saying, "Thus saith the king, Let not Hezekiah deceive you : for he shall not be able to deliver you out of his hand: neither let Hezekiah make you trust in the Lord, saying, The Lord will surely deliver us, and this city shall not be delivered into the hand of the king of Assyria. Hearken not to Hezekiah; for thus saith the king of Assyria, Make an agreement with me, by a present, and come out to me, and then eat ye every man of his own vine, and every one of his fig-tree, and drink ye every one his waters of his cistern: until I come and take you away to a land like your own land, a land of corn and wine, a land of bread and vineyards, a land of oil-olive and of honey, that ye may live and not die." The people made no answer to this speech, but kept silence; for thus their king had commanded them.   Thereupon Hezekiah himself received a letter from Sennacherib, in which the following language was used: "Let not thy God in whom thou trustest deceive thee, saying, Jerusalem shall not be delivered into the hands of the king of Assyria. "Behold, thou hast heard what the kings of Assyria have done to all lands by destroying them utterly: and shalt thou be delivered?   Have the gods of the nations delivered them which my fathers have destroyed?"   Such was the threatening contents of the letter; the fear and alarm which it caused were great; no means seemed available to ward off the danger.   But what should be done, whenever human help is no longer strong enough to save us? Hezekiah went into the Temple of his God, clothed in garments of penance and mourning, and prayed as follows; "O Lord God of Israel, Thou art the God, even Thou alone, of all the kingdoms of the earth; Thou hast made heaven and earth.   Lord, bow down Thine ear, and hear: open, Lord, Thine eyes, and see: and hear the words of Sennacherib, which hath sent him to reproach the living God.   Of a truth, Lord, the kings of Assyria have destroyed the nations and their lands, and have cast their gods into the fire; for they were no gods, but the work of men's hands, wood and stone: therefore they have destroyed them.   Now, therefore, O Lord our God, I beseech Thee, save Thou us out of his hand, that all the kingdoms of the earth may know that Thou art the Lord God, even Thou only."   The king requested also the prophet Isaiah to intercede with his prayer, and received the following consoling reply: "Be not afraid or dismayed! The king of Assyria shall do no harm unto thee; by the way that he came, by the same shall he return, and shall not come into this city, saith the Eternal." Even during the same night a pestilence broke out in the camp of the Assyrians, so that, in the morning, the earth was covered with multitudes of dead bodies. And Sennacherib, who knelt in prayer before his idol god in the Temple of Nineveh, was slain by his own two sons. Thus God humbles the haughty.

Soon after the destruction of the Assyrian army, Hezekiah fell sick, when Isaiah came to him and said: "Set thine house in order; for thou shalt die!" No sooner had the king heard this announcement, than he wept and prayed to God that he might prolong his life. His tears and prayer were accepted by God. Before Isaiah had left the city, God ordered him to announce to the king, that fifteen years should be added to the days of his life. Isaiah put a lump of figs upon the boil with which Hezekiah suffered, and thus cured him in the course of three days.

The victory over the Assyrian army produced this effect, that the small kingdom of Judah gained fame and respect among the neighboring nations. The king of Babylon sent ambassadors to Hezekiah, to congratulate him upon his recovery. On this occasion, the latter forgot himself, and showed, misled by self-pleasing pride, his vast treasures to the ambassadors. This self-exaltation was followed by the announcement of divine punishment: that all these treasures, together with the king's children, should be carried to Babylon. Hezekiah bowed with humility to the will of God, and received the consoling assurance, that this calamity should not occur during his lifetime. He died lamented by his people, after a reign of twenty-nine years.

66. THE KINGS OF JUDAH. (Continued.) MANASSEH—
AMON — JOSIAH — JEHOAHAZ — JEHOIAKIM—JEHOIACHIN
—ZEDEKIAH. [2 Kings xxi.-xxv. 2 Chr. xxxiii.-xxxvi:]
3377 A.M.

The Destruction of the Kingdom of Judah.

Hezekiah was succeeded by his son *Manasseh*, the most
wicked of all the kings of Judah. He built idolatrous
altars even in the Temple of Jerusalem, kept fortune-
tellers and soothsayers, and sacrificed his own son to
Moloch. Idolatry having become worse in Judah than
among the heathens, God sent prophets to the king, saying: "Behold, I am bringing such evil upon Jerusalem
and Judah that whosoever heareth of it, both his ears
shall tingle. I will deliver them into the hand of their
enemies, and bring heavy distress upon them." But the
people would not heed the words of the prophets, and
God caused the Assyrian king, *Esarhaddon*, to invade the
country, and carry Manasseh in fetters to Babylon. Now
the latter repented; wherefore the All-merciful delivered
him from his captivity, and permitted him to return to
Jerusalem, and resume the royal power. From this time
to his death, Manasseh was pious and God-fearing. He
removed the idols from the Temple, and cast them out of
the city, and urgently admonished his people to worship
the living God. He died after a reign of fifty-five years,
and was succeeded by his son

Amon, who reigned but two years. He led a wicked life,
and was assassinated in his own house. The people avenged
his murder by slaying the rebels, and proclaimed his son

Josiah, a child of only eight years, king of Judah.
Obeying the good counsel of his guardian, the priest *Hil-
kiah*, Josiah reformed the worship of the Temple. On
this occasion, the Book of the Law, which had been given
by Moses, but was forgotten during the existence of the
idolatrous worship, was found and sent to the king. With
astonishment and horror he discovered how often he had
violated the will of God, and what a sad future awaited
him, if he would not walk in His ways. Filled with fear
and grief, he rent his clothes, and consulted the prophetess

Huldah, concerning his fate. Huldah sent him word, saying: "Thus saith the Lord, 'Because thy heart hath been softened by the words of the Law, and thou didst humble thyself before God, thou shalt be gathered to thy fathers in peace, and thine eyes shall not see the evil which I will bring upon this land.'" Josiah now made all possible exertions to restore the worship of the true God. He made the whole people promise, that they would henceforth follow the law of the Lord, and then celebrated, in Jerusalem, the feast of Passover, which had not been solemnized with such splendor since the days of the Judges. After a reign of thirty-one years, he died from a wound which he had received in a war against the Egyptian king Necho.

He was successively followed by his sons *Jehoahaz, Jehoiakim*, and then by *Jehoiachin*, the son of the latter, all of whom re-introduced idolatry, in consequence of which, vice rapidly increased in Judah and accelerated the destruction of the nation. God delivered the people into the hand of *Nebuchadnezzar*, king of Babylon, who carried Jehoiachin, together with ten thousand Jews, the treasures of the Temple, and its golden and silver vessels, to Babylon. In the place of the deposed king, Nebuchadnezzar appointed *Zedekiah*, a son of Josiah, to fill the royal throne. The latter soon rebelled, whereupon Nebuchadnezzar marched against him, and laid siege to the city* with his whole army.

This siege lasted two years. Famine and misery made horrible havoc in the city; its inhabitants fell in the streets dying with destitution and hunger; mothers ate their own children. At last, on the ninth day of the fourth month, the enemy made an attack upon the city and took it. Zedekiah took to flight, but was taken prisoner at Jericho, by the generals of Nebuchadnezzar, who carried him, together with his whole family, before the king. The latter caused his children to be slain before his face, his eyes to be put out, and then sent him in fetters to Babylon, where he died in a prison. The magnificent Temple, the royal palace,

---

* This was done on the tenth day of the month of *Tebet*.

nay, the whole city was burned down, and the walls razed to its very foundation.*

But a limited number of the country people were permitted to remain in Canaan, and had *Gedaliah*, the son of *Ahikan*, appointed over them as governor. Gedaliah ruled with great mildness, and said to his people: "Fear not to be the servants of the Chaldees; dwell in the land, and faithfully serve the king of Babylon; and it shall be well with you." Many of those who had fled, began to flock to Jerusalem, when *Ishmael*, of the royal family, assisted by ten other men, assassinated the governor. Then the remnant of the people, dreading the resentment of the Babylonians, fled to Egypt.†

§ 67. THE PROPHETS JEREMIAH AND EZEKIEL.

At the time of the destruction of Jerusalem, lived the prophets *Jeremiah* and *Ezekiel*.

Jeremiah was the son of a priest who lived at *Anathoth*. God called him to the prophetic work in the thirteenth year of the reign of Josiah. Like Moses in ancient time, Jeremiah unwillingly followed the divine call, deeming himself too young and incapable to fulfill such an important mission. But God removed his scruples by the assurance, that He would be with him, and communicate to him *that* which he should proclaim. Encouraged by this assurance, he stepped before a most obstinate and corrupt people, with the bold courage, with the greatest intrepidity of a glorious hero, to struggle for God and His holy law. He inveighed, without reserve, against the vices of the high and the humble, and admonished them to mend their ways. "Thou shall perish," he said to the apostate king Jehoiakim, "and none shall lament for thee." He prophesied also the destruction of the people, if they would not return to God. They got angry against him for such speeches, and hated him. Once Jeremiah preached again in the court of the Temple against the general corruption of the city, and prophesied woe and misery, and

---

* On the seventh day of *Ab*.
† This event took place in the month of *Tishri*.

the complete destruction of the city and Temple, unless
they would speedily repent. Then the whole assembly,
the priests and false prophets, exclaimed : " This man must
die!"—seized the prophet of the Lord, and carried him
before the court of the princes.   Jeremiah addressed them,
saying: " Behold, I am in your hand: do with me as it
seemeth good and right in your eyes.   Only forget not,
that if ye put me to death. ye shall surely bring innocent
blood upon yourselves.   The Lord hath sent me unto you
to speak all these words in your ears.   Therefore, now
mend your ways and your doings, and God will avert the
evil that he hath pronounced against you."   Then the princes
and many of the people exclaimed : " This man deserveth
not that he should die."   But *Urijah*, another prophet,
who prophesied like Jeremiah, was indeed put to death,
upon the order of king Jehoiakim, and his body thrown
into the graves of the common people.

Jeremiah went to his native place but even there he
was persecuted on account of his open speeches.   He was
compelled to leave his paternal home and inheritance, and
seek his safety in flight.   When he had again arrived at
Jerusalem, he preached in the streets and market-places,
and exhorted the people to repentance.   Then a priest
smote him in the face; the people laughed at him ; he
was thrown into a dungeon, where he began to reflect
whether, the people being so stiff-necked, it were not better to be silent than to speak.   " But," exclaims the inspired prophet, " a burning desire was shut up in my bones,
and I was weary with forbearing, and I could not keep
silent."   Thus he continued to fulfill his important mission.

He wrote also a letter to the Israelites in Babylon, who
had been carried thither after the first capture of Jerusalem, containing the following admonition: " Thus saith
the Lord of hosts, the God of Israel, unto all that are carried away captives, whom I have caused to be carried
away from Jerusalem unto Babylon : build ye houses, and
dwell in them ; and plant gardens, and eat the fruit of
them ; and seek the peace of the city whither I have caused
you to be carried away captives, and pray unto the Lord
for it: for in the peace thereof shall ye have peace.   For
thus saith the Lord of hosts, the God of Israel ; Let not

your prophets and your diviners, that be in the midst of you, deceive you, neither hearken to your dreams which ye cause to be dreamed. For they prophesy falsely unto you in my name: I have not sent them, saith the Lord. For thus saith the Lord, That after seventy years be accomplished at Babylon, I will visit you, and perform my good word toward you, in causing you to return to this place. For I know the thoughts that I think toward you, saith the Lord, thoughts of peace, and not of evil, to give you an expected end: and I will turn away your captivity, and I will gather you from all the nations, and from all the places whither I have driven you, saith the Lord; and I will bring you again into the place whence I caused you to be carried away captive." And when king Zedekiah went to Babylon to do homage to the Babylonian ruler, Jeremiah handed *Seraiah*, one of the princes who accompanied Zedekiah, a book containing exhortations and prophecies for the Babylonian Jews. Seraiah secretly read it to them, then bound it to a stone, and cast it into the river Euphrates; he did so, no doubt, that it should not excite any suspicion among the Babylonians.

But Jeremiah himself remained in Caanan, although he knew that the land would soon be visited by heavy calamities. He would not desert his people under any circumstances, but was resolved to stand by them to the last hour, and use all means to induce them to repentance. The less his admonitions were heeded, the more powerfully would he inveigh against the sins of his people. Once he entered the court of the royal palace with a wooden yoke on his neck. when another prophet approached him and broke the yoke. But Jeremiah said: "The yoke of the people shall be turned into an iron yoke." But when he was about to leave Jerusalem, through the gate of Benjamin, a captain of the guard, supposing that he intended to join the enemy. took him and put him in prison in the castle of Zion. Here he bought from one of his relatives a piece of land situated at Anathoth—just at the time when the Chaldees besieged the city, and there was no prospect of their defeat by the Judeans. By this act he meant to indicate to his brethren, that, however great their distress was, and how certain their destruction, they should again.

possess the land of their fathers. King Zedekiah alleviated
the burthen of his imprisonment; but when he continued
to advise subjection to the Chaldees, the captains of the
Israelites grew indignant, and cast him into a pit filled
with mire, in which he would certainly have perished, had
not the king, upon hearing thereof, ordered his servant to
take him up. But he was again put into prison, where he
remained until Jerusalem was taken.

It might be supposed that the final capture of the city
filled the prophet with delight, because he was now delivered from all persecution; but such a feeling did not
enter his bosom. He wept tears of bitter grief over the
great calamity of his people, and poured forth the deep
anguish of his soul in affecting elegies, which constitute a
portion of the Bible, known as the "*Lamentations of
Jeremiah.*"

King Nebuchadnezzar sent word to Jeremiah, saying:
"Behold, I loose thee this day from the chains which were
upon thine hand. If it seem good unto thee to come with
me into Babylon, come; and I will look well unto thee;
but if it seem ill unto thee to come with me into Babylon,
forbear; behold, all the land is before thee; whither it
seemeth good and convenient for thee to go, thither go;"
But Jeremiah preferred to remain with his unhappy brethren, to and alleviate their misery. He supported Gedaliah,
the governor of Judah, and when, after the murder of the
latter, the Israelites went to Egypt, they forced him to
accompany them. But even here he found no rest; for
the Jews again committed idolatry, and however urgently
he exhorted and rebuked them, he could not succeed. Nay,
they distinctly declared to him, that they would not obey
the word of God. And thus they hastened toward their
perdition. Of Jeremiah's further history nothing is known.

Contemporaneously with Jeremiah lived the prophets
Zephaniah and *Ezekiel.* Ezekiel was carried to Babylon,
by Nebuchadnezzar, with other Jewish captives under
king Jehoiachin. While living near the Babylonian river
Chebar, God appointed him a prophet unto his brethren.
His mission was, like that of Jeremiah, to admonish the
Judeans to repentance, and to proclaim the approaching
destruction of the kingdom. But he, too, was opposed by

false prophets, who induced the people not to give ear to the exhortations of Ezekiel. But the Israelites learned too soon the truth of his predictions. They heard of the destruction of the empire, began to respect the words of the prophets of God, and to place implicit confidence in their announcements of the speedy return to their native country.

E. The History of the Israelites during, and after the Babylonian Captivity.

§ 68. DANIEL—HANANIAH—MISHAEL—AND AZARIAH.—

The Jews whom Nebuchadnezzar had carried to Babylon, were not kept like prisoners, but were free, and could even acquire fields; only their return to their country was interdicted. But what they were mostly grieved at, was this, that they could no longer worship their God as they had done at Jerusalem; for in Babylon they had no temple, no priests, no teachers. Their calamities, however, conduced to their improvement: they began to reflect, and now, amid heathen nations, they showed not the least inclination to idolatry. Many were even ready to suffer death rather than violate the holy law of God. Among these were *Daniel, Hananiah, Mishael,* and *Azariah.* The king had ordered that these youths, who were of royal descent, should be instructed in arts and sciences, and receive their provisions from his own table. But they refused to partake of the costly viands, (because they deemed it unlawful to eat of the viands of idolaters,) and asked only for pulse and water. Nevertheless, they appeared healthier and more cheerful than others who had partaken of the royal viands; for their moderation in food and drink, together with the joyful emotions of a good conscience, preserved their health. But also in knowledge and wisdom they surpassed other youths, so that the king soon took them into his own service, and raised them to the highest dignities.

But the time of trial also came for them. King Nebuchadnezzar had a large golden image, an idol of Baal erected, and decreed that all persons should worship it,

and that every one who would not obey his order, should
be thrown into a burning fiery furnace. All fell down and
adored the idol; but the three last named youths refused
to do so; wherefore the king commanded that they should
suffer the penalty pronounced for such disobedience. But
God delivered them in a wonderful way, and Nebuchadnezzar exclaimed, saying: "Blessed be the God of Hananiah, Mishael, and Azariah, who hath delivered His servants that trusted in Him, and yielded their bodies, that
they might not serve nor worship any god, except their
own God! Therefore, this is my decree: Whoever speaketh
any thing amiss against this God, shall be cut in pieces,
and his house shall be laid waste, because there is no other
God that can deliver like unto this God."

Daniel also gave proofs of his impregnable attachment
to God. He was honored and loved, not only by Nebuchadnezzar, but also by *Darius*, one of his successors: a
circumstance which caused the envy of many who endeavored to bring him into disgrace at the royal court.
Unable to discover any thing wrong in his conduct—for
his loyalty was unexceptionable—they procured from the
king an edict, that no one should offer up prayers to God
for the space of thirty days; and that every violater of this
decree should be thrown into a den of hungry lions. Daniel
did not heed this decree, but continued to pray to his God,
and thus the king was compelled, as he could not evade
his own decree, to have his favorite thrown into the lion's
den. But All-merciful God so ordained it, that the lions
would not do him the least injury. The king, deeply
grieved on account of Daniel, could neither eat nor sleep,
and hastened very early in the morning to the lion's den,
to see what had become of him. When he found him alive,
he commanded that he should be taken from the den, and
those thrown into it, who had accused his faithful favorite.
Before they had reached the bottom of the den, the lions
devoured them all. The king was greatly astonished, and
decreed, that all the inhabitants of his land should adore
the God of Daniel, because he was the only true God.
Thenceforth Daniel remained the favorite of the king, and
lived even to the first year of the reign of *Koresh*, (Cyrus.)
He gained the favor of several kings of Babylon, especially

by his skillful interpretations of mysterious dreams. He had himself spiritual visions, which are related in that book of Holy Writ, which bears his own name. However, he is not recognized as a prophet.

---

§ 69.   The Return of the Jews from the Babylonian Captivity.   [Ezra i-vi.]   3446 A.M.

Seventy years had the Jews passed in captivity, when the Persian king *Cyrus,* who had conquered Babylon, granted them permission to return to their own country, and rebuild their national temple. Many of the captives, however, did not avail themselves of this permission, but remained in Babylon, where they had acquired lands, and adopted the customs of the country. About fifty thousand of the people, among them two hundred singers, returned to Jerusalem, led by *Zerubbabel,* a descendant of the kings of Judah, and the priest *Jeshua,* who became afterwards high-priest. Those that remained presented their returning brethren with rich gifts, and king Cyrus himself delivered to them five thousand four hundred sacred vessels which had been taken from the temple. Inspiring themselves by songs of joy, they accomplished their journey, and, after having taken possession of cities and villages, they assembled again on the first day of the seventh month, at Jerusalem, erected an altar upon the ruins of the Temple and offered up sacrifices. When, the year following, the foundation was laid for the rebuilding of the Temple, the priests were present, attired with their official garments, and with trumpets in their hands, and the Levites with cymbals, to praise God, together with the people: "And they sang together in choirs, praising and giving thanks unto the Lord; because he is good, for His mercy endureth forever toward Israel. And all the people shouted with a great shout, when they praised the Lord, because the foundation of the house of the Lord was laid. But many of the priests and Levites, and chief of the fathers, who were ancient men, that had seen the first house, when the foundation of this house was laid before their eyes, wept with a loud voice; and many shouted aloud for joy:

so that the people could not discern the noise of the shout of joy from the noise of the weeping of the people: for the people shouted with a loud shout, and the noise was heard afar off."

Now, when the Samaritans, the enemies of Judah and Benjamin, heard that the Jews builded a temple unto the Eternal, they came to Zerubbabel, and to the chief of the fathers, and said unto them: "Let us build with you; for we seek your God, as ye do." But Zerubbabel, and Jeshua, and the chief of the rest of the fathers, replied: "Ye have nothing to do with us to build a house unto our God; we will alone build it, as king Cyrus had commanded us." On account of this refusal, the Samaritans endeavored to prevent and disturb the re-erection of the Temple. They brought calumnies against the Jews before the king, and succeeded so far, by bribing the royal officers in Persia, that the work of building was interrupted till the death of Cyrus, and distinctly prohibited by his successor *Artachshashta.*

---

§ 70.   HAGGAI AND ZECHARIAH.   [Book of Haggai i. and ii.   Zechariah iv. viii. ix.   Ezra v. vi.]

Thus the holy work remained interrupted for fifteen years. The people had lost the necessary courage and zeal for its continuation; yet they inhabited beautiful houses; their continual attention to worldly affairs gradually caused their zeal for the service of God to abate, so that the work perhaps would never have been resumed, if God had not admonished them through famine, want of the means of subsistence, and other chastisements, but above all, through the prophets *Haggai* and *Zechariah.*

It was in the second year of the reign of king Darius, when the word of the Lord came unto *Zerubbabel,* governor of Judah, through the medium of Haggai, the prophet, saying: " This people say, The time is not come, the time that the Lord's house should be built. Is it time for you, O ye, to dwell in your cieled houses, and this house lie waste? Now, therefore, thus saith the Lord of hosts: Consider your ways. Ye have sown much, and bring in little;

ye eat, but ye have not enough; ye drink, but ye are not filled with drink: ye clothe you, but there is none warm; and he that earneth wages earneth wages to put it into a bag with holes. Thus saith the Lord of hosts: Consider your ways. Go up to the mountain and bring wood, and build the house; and I will take pleasure in it, and I will be glorified, saith the Lord."

Now Zerubbabel, and Jeshua, the high priest, and all the people obeyed the voice of the Eternal, their God. All came and laid hand to the work in the house of the Lord of hosts, their God.

The prophet *Zechariah* also, upon the command of God, encouraged Zerubbabel and the people, to continue the holy work.

At the same time, *Tatnai*, the Persian governor, came to Jerusalem with his companions, and asked the Jews, seeing them build their temple: "Who has permitted you to build this house?" They answered· "King Cyrus." Hereupon the governor wrote to king Darius, requesting to inquire into the matter, whether such permission had been given the Jews. Inquiry was made, and a roll, which contained the decree of king Cyrus, concerning the rebuilding of the Temple, having been found, the governors of the king were instructed not only not to hinder the work of the Jews, but even to assist them, and defray all necessary expenses from the royal treasury; the sacrifices also should be furnished to them, that they could pray to their God for the life of the king and of his sons.

Thus the work was finished after four years. The consecration of the Temple was then celebrated with great joy and exultation; "for God had made them joyful, and turned the heart of the king unto them."

§ 71. ESTHER.

The history of the Jews who remained in Persia, contains an event which teaches us anew, how God's providence watches over the destinies of man.

After the death of king Cyrus, *Ahasuerus* ascended the royal throne. Under his reign, there lived at *Shushan*, the

capital of the kingdom, a Jew, whose name was *Mordecai,*
and who had adopted and educated *Esther,* the daughter
of his uncle, because she had neither father nor mother.
Esther was pious and beautiful, and pleased the king so
much, that he chose her for his wife.   But she told no one
that she was a Jewess; for thus had Mordecai charged
her.   Mordecai went every morning to the gate of the
royal palace to inquire after her welfare.   Once he overheard
two chamberlains, as they conspired to slay the king.
Faithful to his king, he informed him, through Esther, of
the conspiracy.   The matter was investigated, and the information being found correct, the two chamberlains were
hanged, and the name of Mordecai recorded, together with
the narrative of the event, in the chronicles of the empire.

At that time, a certain *Haman* was the king's favorite.
Now, this Haman was greatly displeased with Mordecai,
because he would not bend his knee before him.   "This
homage," thought Mordecai, "I can pay only to my God."
For this reason, Haman resolved to take revenge, but not
upon Mordecai alone, but upon all his brethren, and to
carry out his design, he advised the king to destroy the
Jews; "for," said he, "this people is scattered, yet separated among the nations in all the provinces of thy kingdom; and their laws are different from those of every
people, while they do not execute the laws of the king;
and it is no profit for the king to tolerate them.   If it be
pleasing to the king, let a decree be written to destroy
them, and ten thousand talents of silver will I weigh out
into the king's treasuries.   The king yielded, and a decree
was at once sent to all the provinces of the empire, "to
destroy, to kill, and to exterminate all the Jews, from
young to old, little ones, men and women, on one day, the
thirteenth day of the twelfth month, *Adar,* and to plunder
their property as spoil."

When Mordecai heard this, he rent his clothes, wept
and lamented, and informed Esther of the designs of Haman, and admonished her, at the same time, to address
the king and implore his grace for her people.   But alas!
she, like all the king's subjects, could not approach him
uncalled, at the penalty of death.   Yet, her love for her
people was so strong, that she risked her life.   For three

days she fasted and prayed, and with her all her brethren; and then she appeared before the king. As soon as he saw her, he rose, extended his hand to her, and asked her what she desired. She answered: "If it please the king, let the king and Haman come this day unto the banquet that I have prepared for him." This request, the only one which Esther uttered, was granted. At the table, the king was in such good humor that he permitted the queen to ask some favor. And she requested the king and Haman "to come to another banquet which she would prepare for to-morrow." Full of joy and pleasure, Haman left the royal palace. But when he again saw Mordecai at the king's gate, "who did not rise up nor move out of his way," he said to his wife, after telling her of the honor and glory lavished upon him by the queen: "Yet, all this profiteth me nothing, as long as I see that Jew Mordecai sitting in the king's gate. He then resolved to erect a gallows, fifty cubits high, to hang Mordecai thereon in the morning.

In that same night it so happened, that the king could not sleep, and he ordered, with a view of whiling away the time, that the books of the memorable events of the chronicles should be brought before him, and passages read from them. On this occasion the king heard again of the conspiracy of the two chamberlains, and was greatly astonished also to learn, that Mordecai had never been rewarded for his loyalty.

In the morning Haman entered the king's palace very early, to crave his permission for hanging Mordecai upon the gallows. When the king heard that Haman was in the court, he called him in, and asked him: "What shall be done unto the man whom the king desireth to honor?" The vain and ambitious Haman, thinking that the king could allude to no man but himself, replied: "For the man whom the king delighteth to honor, let the royal apparel be brought which the king useth to wear, and the horse that the king rideth upon, and the crown royal which is set upon his head: and let this apparel and horse be delivered to the hand of one of the king's most noble princes, that they may array the man withal whom the king delighteth to honor, and bring him on horseback through the streets of the city, and proclaim before him. Thus shall it be done to the man whom the king delighteth to honor." "Well spoken," said the king, "make haste, and do this to Mordecai, the Jew that sitteth at the king's gate; leave out nothing of all that thou hast spoken." Haman was obliged to obey. Having faithfully executed the order of the king, he returned home, in sadness, and with his head covered, and there related what had happened, No sooner had he concluded his narrative, than the king's servants came to conduct him to the queen's banquet.

At table the king remembered his promise, and asked Esther again: "What wilt thou, and what is thy request? and were it even half of the kingdom, it should still be given thee!" Then Esther the queen answered and said: "If I have found favor in thy sight, O king, and if it please the king, let my life be given me at my petition, and my people at my request; for we are sold, I and my people, to be destroyed, to be slain, and to perish."

·To the question of the king, "Who is it, and where is he, whose heart has emboldened him to do so?" Esther replied; "An adversary—that cruel man—this wicked Haman!"

Haman became so terrified that he could not endure the looks of the king and queen. But the king became enraged against him, and, when one of his servants told him that Haman had prepared a gallows for Mordecai, who had saved the king's life, he ordered that *Haman* should be hanged thereon, and Mordecai receive his place. And the decree, to destroy the Jews on one day, was not executed. On that day, there was some fighting between their enemies and the Jews, but the latter were victorious, and the following day was a day of joy and festival for them. Even many heathens embraced their religion. In commemoration of this event, the Jews celebrate, even to this day, on the fourteenth of *Adar*, the annual Feast of *Purim*—that is, *Lots*, so called, because Haman had cast lots for fixing the day of the extermination of the Jews, and God changed it to their advantage.

72. Ezra and Nehemiah.

Under the reign of *Artaxerxes*, the priest and scribe *Ezra* also left Babylon and went to Jerusalem, accompanied by many priests, Levites, singers, and other ministers of the Temple, together with more than one thousand seven hundred persons, to promote the affairs of his brethren. The military escort offered to him by his king, he would not accept; "for," said he, "God is my Shield and Protection." He carried, however, a letter of the king with him, containing the royal order, that the province of Babylon should, as the king had done, assist Ezra by contributions of money, and that the latter was vested with the power of teaching the law, and appointing magistrates and judges.

When Ezra arrived at Jerusalem he perceived, to his profound grief, that the Jews did manifest but little zeal in the fulfillment of their religious obligations, and especially that many of them, and among them even priests and Levites, had married heathen women. In his grief he rent his clothes, plucked off the hair of his head and beard, and sat down, solitary, and absorbed in meditations how things could be improved. In the evening he assembled the people, offered up most fervent prayers, and admonished them to mend their ways. The people were moved, and the better ones exclaimed: "Yes, we have trespassed against our God; yet, let us make a new Covenant with God—we are with thee!" Ezra then admonished them to come again to Jerusalem on the third day, that they might deliberate together upon further measures. Numerous was the assembly, notwithstanding the heavy rain which then fell; they resolved and solemnly vowed to send away their heathen wives, and henceforth remain faithful to their God.

When Ezra thus labored in Jerusalem, another pious Israelite, *Nehemiah*, held the office of cup-bearer at the court of king Artaxerxes. When he learned that his brethren, who had returned to Jerusalem, lived in want and misery, that the walls of the city were still in ruins, and its gates not yet rebuilt, he wept, prayed, and fasted, his cheeks grew hollow, and his whole countenance bore the marks of profound woe and grief. The king observed

this, and asked him: "Why is thy countenance sad?"
To which Nehemiah replied: "Why should not my countenance be sad, when the city, the place of my fathers'
sepulchres, lieth waste, and the gates thereof are consumed
with fire." Then said the king: "For what dost thou make
request?" Nehemiah replied: "If it please the king, and
if thy servant have found favor in thy sight, that thou
wouldest send me unto Judah, to assist my brethren."
The king granted Nehemiah's request, and gave him, moreover, letters to the governors, ordering them to provide
the Jews with timber for their work, and protect them in
its execution. Arrived at Jerusalem, Nehemiah admonished
all the Jews to be zealous and industrious, and encouraged
them by his own example. But *Sanballat*, a Samaritan,
and other adversaries of the Jews, laughed them to scorn,
and said: "What is this thing that ye do? it appears that
ye intend to rebel against the king." And *Tobiah*, another
of their enemies, said: "Let them but build: if a fox go
up, he shall even break down their stone wall." The Jews
did not heed these speeches, but continued their work
with increased zeal; "every one with one of his hands
wrought in the work, and with the other hand held a
weapon." Thus they completed the walls in fifty-two days.

Soon after, there was great famine in the land, and many
Israelites came to Nehemiah and said: "We, our sons,
and our daughters, are many; therefore we take up corn
for them, that we may eat, and live. We have mortgaged
our lands, vineyards, and houses, that we might buy corn,
because of the dearth. We have borrowed money for the
king's tribute, and that upon our lands and vineyards.
Yet now our flesh is as the flesh of our brethren, our children as their children: and lo, we bring into bondage our
sons and our daughters to be servants, and some of our
daughters are brought unto bondage already: neither is
it in our power to redeem them; for other men have our
lands and vineyards." When Nehemiah heard these com-
plaints, he rebuked the nobles, and the rulers, and said:
"Will ye exact usury of your brethren? Should ye not
walk in the fear of our God because of the reproach
of the heathen, our enemies?" Then they answered:
"We will restore them every thing, and will require

nothing of them." Nehemiah himself, although royal governor, took no salary, and led a very frugal life, that the people might not be burthened with taxes: nor would he allow his servants to oppress them. Every day he invited one hundred and fifty men to his own table, and showed himself the best pattern for all.

When the external security was established, the people assembled at Jerusalem, that they might hear the law, which Ezra read to them from morning until mid-day. He stood upon a kind of pulpit, while the people remained standing until he had concluded. He then thanked and praised God, the Holy One of Israel, and all the people answered: "Amen! Amen!" Afterwards, they made a solemn vow to be faithful to the laws of their God, and affirmed it by signing a written covenant.

Soon after, Nehemiah was compelled to return to his king, but when he came back to Jerusalem, he found, to his deep mortification, that his arrangements had but partially been complied with. Even *Manasseh*, a priest, refused to send away his heathen wife, the daughter of *Sanballat*, the Samaritan, so that Nehemiah was compelled to banish him from the country.

This religious lukewarmness on the part of the Jews, called forth the rebukes of *Malachi*, the last of the prophets. He severely reproved his brethren who would marry heathen women, refused to pay the tithes, and neglected the service of God ; and his words seem to have produced the desired effect.

---

§ 73. FURTHER EVENTS IN THE HISTORY OF THE JEWS.

The Jews gradually multiplied again, spread over the country, and lived peaceful and contented under the rule of the Persian kings, who placed governors over them, while their priests possessed, as in former times, the highest power in their spiritual affairs, and afterwards obtained even some authority with regard to the management of their civil concern. After the conquest of Persia by *Alexander the Great*, the Judeans became the subjects of this illustrious prince. After his death, and the division of his empire, they lived, for almost a century, under the rule of the kings of *Egypt*, the *Ptolemies*, and then under that of the *Syrian* kings. During the reign of all these kings, they were entirely free and independent, with regard both to their religious and civil affairs; they had only to pay a fixed tribute. But things changed under the Syrian king *Antiochus Epiphanes*. He treated the Jews with great cruelty; he captured Jerusalem, took the sacred vessels, slew men, women and children, and made all efforts to make the Jews idolaters.

As an instance of his atrocious cruelty, let us listen to the following narrative. He ordered a mother with her seven sons to be brought before him, and to be tortured, in order thus to force them to forsake their religion. But neither threat nor promise could move them. "There is another life," said the pious mother, "lasting longer than the present; though they take this life, which is but short, the Lord shall give us another—far better one—lasting unto eternity." Joyfully did the sons endure the most horrible tortures, and one after the other met his death with the most astonishing courage; and after all of them, their noble-hearted and virtuous mother willingly submitted to be made a victim of her faithfulness to her God and religion.

Antiochus sent messengers also to the priest *Mattathias*, to induce him to apostasy. With contempt he refused their offers, collected a faithful band around him, and succeeded so far with them and his five sons, of whom *Judah Maccabi* was the most gallant, that he could defy the king's haughtiness. Some time afterwards, Antiochus set out to go in person to Jerusalem and subjugate the Jews. But he fell from his chariot, and was taken dangerously ill. Now he promised to improve. But it was of no avail; his sufferings increased; while yet alive, his body decayed, worms grew upon him, and the odor near him was intolerable. At last he died under the greatest agonies.

In the mean while, Judah Maccabi entered Jerusalem, cleansed the temple, re-erected the altar, and celebrated with his brethren, during eight days, the *Feast of Dedication,* which is still observed every year in Israel.

Thus the Jews were again free, and lived in peace and concord. The descendants of Matthatias became the kings of the new Jewish Commonwealth, which was, in later times, again visited by strifes and contentions. Several religious sects grew into existence; hatred and discord went on increasing, the nation was separated in parties, and the Roman General, *Pompey*, was requested by one of the Maccabean family to afford him aid. Thus the land of the Jews was made tributary to the Roman empire. By the aid of the Romans, *Herod*, the Edomite, ascended the throne of Judea, but was so cruel and ambitious, that he brought great misery upon his people. Still worse fared the Jews after his death, when Roman governors ruled over them with such intolerable cruelty, as to excite them to rebellion. Now, *Nero*, the emperor of Rome, sent *Vespasian*, and his son *Titus* to Judea, to quell the rebellion. After the most terrible struggles, Jerusalem and the Temple were at last destroyed, and the Jewish people dispersed over all parts of the earth. From that time. Israel has ceased to be an independent nation, and the Jews are in duty bound to regard and love that land wherein they live, as their home and country, to obey its laws, and to promote the welfare of all their fellow-citizens, without distinction of creed and denomination.

APPENDIX.

A Brief Outline of the Geography of Canaan.

I.

Canaan—called also *Palestine*, the *Land of Judah*, the *Land of Israel*, the *Promised Land*, the *Holy Land*—forms a portion of Asia, and covers an area of about eighteen thousand seven hundred and fifty square miles. It is bounded on the East by the Arabian desert, on the South, by Arabia and Egypt, on the West, by the Mediterranean Sea, and on the North, by Phœnicia and Syria.

II.

Canaan is a *mountainous* country—"a land of hills and valleys." Of its mountains we mention: 1. *Lebanon* and *Anti-Lebanon*, the south-eastern continuation of which is called *Hermon*. 2. The *Mountains of Naphtali*. 3. Mount *Carmel*. 4. Mount *Tabor*. 5. Mount *Gilboa*. 6. The *Mountains of Ephraim, or Israel*—of which the following points are noted, namely: *Zalmon*, *Gerizim*, *Ebal*, and *Gaash*. 7. The *Mountains of Judea*, with Mount *Carmel*, (not to be mistaken for Mount Carmel mentioned under No. 3,) and the Mount of *Olives*. 8. The *Mountains of Gilead*. 9. The *Abarim* Mountains, with Mount *Peor* and Mount *Nebo*.

III.

Although Palestine is very mountainous, it contains nevertheless, some *Plains* or *Level* regions. Such are: The *Plain of Jezreel;* the *Plain of Sharon*, near Mount Carmel; the *Plain of Jordan;* the *Plain of Jericho;* the *Plain of Moab*.

IV.

The most noted *Valleys* of Palestine are the following: The *Valley of Salt ;* the *Valley of Kidron;* the *Valley of Gerar;* the *Valley of Hinnom;* the *Valley of Rephaim*, and the *Valley of Eshcol*.

V.

The Bible mentions, also, *Deserts* of Canaan. Those most known are: The *Wilderness of Judea*, connected with the wildernesses of Engedi, Ziph, and Maon; the *Wilderness of Beer-Sheba*.

VI.

The principal river of Palestine is the *Jordan*. Rising at the foot of Mount Hermon, it traverses the country from north to south, to an extent of ninety miles, and empties into the Dead Sea. The *Kishon* comes from Mount Tabor, and flows into one of the bays of the Mediterranean Sea. The *Arnon* rises from the Arabian Mountains, and empties into the Dead Sea. The *Jabbok*, near the boundaries of the Ammonites, flows into the Jordan. The *Kidron*, near Jerusalem, empties into the Dead Sea.

VII.

There are three renowned Lakes in Canaan: 1. The *Sea of Chinnereth*, (called also the *Sea of Galilee*, and *Sea of Tiberias*.) 2. The *Sea of Merom*. 3. The *Salt Sea*, (called, also, the *Dead Sea*, *Lake Asphaltites*, and the *Sea of the Plain*.)

VIII.

Of the *Mineral Waters* of Canaan we may mention: The *Warm Baths of Tiberias;* the Mineral Springs of Kallirrhooe, near Macherus; the sulphur springs of Gadara.

On account of the want of water-wells, cisterns were used in Palestine, to gather and keep rain-water in them

IX.

The *climate* of Palestine is mild. In ancient times, the year was divided in *Six Seasons*. The first season, *Seedtime*, lasted from the middle of October to the middle of December, and is distinguished by the "early rain," (*yoreh;*) the second or *Winter* season, lasted from the middle of December to the middle of February; the third, *Spring.* lasted from the middle of February to the middle of April, during which time, the so-called "latter rain" (*malkosh*) fell. The fourth season, *Harvest-time*, lasted from the middle of April to the middle of June; the fifth closed in the middle of August; and the sixth, in the middle of October.

X.

With the climate of the country, the *Mode of Dressing* of the inhabitants, which was very simple, is naturally connected. The shirt, called *Tunic*, was bound round the waist with a girdle. The garment over the tunic, was a kind of cloak, and formed, in front, a *"bosom,"* or large fold, which was used for carrying various burdens. The head was covered by a piece of fine cloth, laid in folds, in the shape of a turban. As a covering for the feet, simple *soles* (*sandals*) were used, which were fastened with straps around the foot and ankle. For journeys, a second *Upper Garment* was used, and served during night, both for a cover and hammock.

The dress of women differed from that of men. Women could never be without their *veils*; and most precious ornaments, such as *bracelets, necklaces* and *finger-rings* were by no means rare articles.

XI.

In former times, Palestine *was* a very fertile country, and distinguished as "a land flowing with milk and honey." The plains and valleys presented ever-blooming gardens; the greatest number of the mountains were most carefully cultivated.

The chief productions of the land were various kinds of *grains, leguminous plants, garden vegetables, flowers, spices,* and a vast number of the most cultivated species of *trees.* Among all these we may mention, as the most noted, wheat, barley, lentils, beans, cumin, flax, cotton, the olive-tree, the cypress-tree, the pomegranate-tree, the fig-tree, the myrrh-tree, the terebinth, the oak, the fir, the zakkum-tree, the carob-tree, the palm, the cedar, and the sugar-tree. The vine grew in luxuriant abundance. Of tame animals, the following among others, deserve particular notice: the sheep, the goat, and other domesticated animals; the ass, the camel, and dogs; also different kinds of poultry. Of wild beasts, Palestine produced bears, lions, wolves, foxes, jackals, unicorns, crocodiles, ostriches, gazelles, chamois, stags and deer.

XII.

Canaan was sometimes visited by the following *Plagues:* Earthquakes, destructive east-winds, hail, locusts, pestilence, drought, devastating rain-showers.

XIII.

The *Cities* of Palestine had very narrow streets, (of but four cubits in width,) and were without pavement. Even Jerusalem received its pavement only under the reign of Agrippa II. The greater cities had extensive market-places near their gates, and very high walls, (forts,) with towers and breastworks. The gates were often overlaid with iron, copper, or brass, ("brazen gates,") The houses were built of rough stone or brick; palaces, of square-stone and marble. The house presented a square figure, had a spacious *court*, which was generally without covering; only now and then a curtain was drawn over it, to keep off the burning sun. Round this court ran the hall, with cisterns for bathing. The *roofs* of the houses were flat and surrounded by a battlement. The *furniture* of a house was scanty. Stoves were unknown; during severe weather, a moveable chimney was used, in which burned a coal-fire, or stood a pot filled with burning char-coal. The houses had no windows, but were provided either with *lattice-work*, or curtains of net work. The doors were barred with wooden bolts; only prisons and other public edifices were provided with iron locks.

XIV.

After having conquered Canaan, Joshua divided the land among the twelve tribes.

On this side of the Jordan lived, from the South to the North, the tribes of Judah, Simon, Benjamin, Dan, Ephraim, Half of the tribe of Manasseh, Asher, Issachar, Zebulun, Naphtali. Beyond the Jordan dwelt the tribes of Reuben, Gad, and Half of Manasseh.

During the rule of the Romans in Palestine, the land was divided into the provinces of Judea, Samaria, Galilee, and Peræa.

Judea, the most southern province, contained the following cities: Jerusalem, Gaza, Joppa, Jericho, Jamnia, Lachish, Adullam, Eglon, Hebron, Tekoa, Mizpah, Gibeon, Gilgal, Ramah.

Samaria, which bounded Judea on the North, had the following cities: Samaria, (Shomeron,) Shiloh, Bethel, Sichem, Thebez, Dotham, Gilgal, Tirzah, Bezek.

In *Galilee*, the most northern province, we find the following cities: Shumen, Endor, Megiddo, Tiberia, Kedesh, Dan.

Peræa, (the land east of the Jordan, Gilead, Bashan,) had the following cities: Aroer, Baal-Meon, Shittim, Heshbon, Mahanaim.

XV.

The *neighboring nations and countries* of Palestine were: 1. The *Phœnicians*, whom the Israelites called *Canaanites*. 2. The *Philistines*, with the cities of Askalon, Ashdod, Gaza, Ekron, Gath. 3. The *Amalekites*, to the south of the former, who descended from one of Esau's grandsons. 4. The *Midianites*, who inhabited the region from Sinai to the Arabian Sea. 5. The *Edomites*, descendants from Edom or Esau, with the following cities: Selah, Bozrah, Masrekah, Teman, and the sea-ports of Elath and Eziongeber. 6. The *Moabites*, to the East of the Dead Sea with the city of Zoar. 7. The *Amorites* and *Ammonites*, to the north of Moab. 8. *Syria*, to the north-east of Palestine, comprised several countries, of which we may mention: *Mesopotomia*. (Aram-Naharim, Padam Aram,) Aram-Zobah, and Aram-Damesek. To the south of Mesopotamia we find *Babylon* on the Euphrates, and *Assyria* on the Tigris, with its capital, *Nineveh*. Further to the east we find *Media* and *Persia*, with their capitals *Ecbatana* and *Shushan*.

INDEX.

I. Primeval History of the Human Race.

Page

§ 1. The Creation of the World 3
§ 2. The First Sin 4
§ 3. Cain and Abel 6
§ 4. Noah 7
§ 5. Noah's departure from the Ark . . . 8
§ 6. The Descendants of Noah 10

II. The Patriarchs.

§ 7. Abraham the Progenitor of the Israelitish Nation 11
§ 8. Abraham showing his Peaceful Disposition
and his Generosity 12
§ 9. Abraham, the Man of Faith 13
§ 10. Abraham, the Hospitable and Compassionate
Patriarch 14
§ 11. The Destruction of Sodom and Gomorrah . 16
§ 12. Abraham's Obedience 16
§ 13. Abraham's Paternal Solicitude for his Son Isaac 18
§ 14. Isaac 19
§ 15. Jacob and Esau 20
§ 16. Jacob's Journey to Haran 21
§ 17. Jacob's Sojourn with Laban 23
§ 18. Jacob's Return to his Native Country . . 24
§ 19. The Brothers of Joseph selling him from Envy 26
§ 20. Joseph a Slave 27
§ 21. Joseph in Prison. 28
§ 22. The release of Joseph 29
§ 23. The First Journey of Joseph's Brothers to Egypt 30
§ 24. The Second Journey of Joseph's Brothers to Egypt 32
§ 25. The Recognition 35
§ 26. The family of Jacob removing to Egypt . 36

III. The Israelites in Egypt.

Page

§ 27. The Birth of Moses 39
§ 28. Moses manifesting his Attachment to his Fellow-
Believers. 40
§ 29 The Appointment of Moses 41
§ 30 The Deliverance of the Israelites from the
Egyptian Bondage 43
§ 31 The Destruction of Pharaoh 45
§ 32. The Proclamation of the Law on Mount Sinai 46
§ 33. The Israelites worshipping the Golden Calf 48
§ 34. Ritual Institutions: The Tabernacle of the Covenant—The Priests—The Levites . . 49
§ 35. The Rebellions of the People, caused by their
Hardships in the Wilderness . . . 52
§ 36. Difficulties arising from Rebellions of Individual
Israelites. 54
§ 37. Wars with Neighboring Nations . . . 55
§ 38. Moses sends Spies into Canaan. The Close of
Israel's Wanderings in the Wilderness . 58
§ 39. Moses' Farewell Address to his People. His Death 59

IV. Israel as a Nation.

A. *Joshua.—The Judges.*

§ 40. Joshua. The Conquest of Canaan . . 62
§ 41. Joshua's Parting Address. His Death . 64
§ 42. The Judges 65
§ 43. The Judges, (*continued*) 66
§ 44. The History of Samson 70
§ 45. Eli and Samuel 73
§ 46. The Sons of Eli 74
§ 47. The Meritorious Acts of Samuel . . . 75
§ 48. God tries and guides the Pious, (Ruth) . 76

B. *The Kings over the Undivided Empire of Israel.*

§ 49. Saul raised to the Royal Throne . . . 78
§ 50. David anointed King over Israel . . . 80
§ 51. Saul persecuting David 82
§ 52. David, King of Israel 85
§ 53. The Rebellion of Absalom.—Death of David 86
§ 54. Solomon 90
§ 55. The Separation of the Kingdom . . . 62

C. *The Kings of Israel*

Page

§ 56. Jeroboam 94
§ 57. The Kings of Israel, (*continued*) Nadab—Baasha
    Elah—Zimr'—)mri—Ahab . . . 95
§ 58. Elijah and Ahau 97
§ 59. Ahaziah—Jehoram. —Jezebel's death . 99
§ 60. The Prophet. Elisha 100
§ 61. The Prophet Jonah 102
§ 62. Job 104
§ 63. The Destruction of the Kingdom of Israel. The
    Prophets 105

D. *The Kings of Judah.*

§ 64. Rehoboam–Abijah–Asa–Jehoshaphat–Jehoram 109
§ 65. The Kings of Judah, (*continued*)–Ahaziah–Je-
    hoash—Amaziah—Uzziah—Jotham—Ahaz-
    Hezekiah 112
§ 66. The Kings of Judah, (*continued*)—Manasseh—
    Amon—Josiah—Jehoahaz—Jehoiakim—Je-
    hoiachin—Zedekiah 116
§ 67. The Prophets Jeremiah and Ezekiel . . 119

E. *The History of the Israelites during and after the Babylonian Captivity.*

§ 68. Daniel—Hannaiah—Mishael—Azariah . 123
§ 69. The Return of the Jews from the Babylonian
    Captivity 125
§ 70. Haggai and Zechariah 126
§ 71. Esther 127
§ 72. Ezra and Nehemiah 131
§ 73. Further Events in the History of the Jews . 133

APPENDIX.

A Brief Outline of the Geography of Canaan . 136

www.ingramcontent.com/pod-product-compliance
Lightning Source LLC
Chambersburg PA
CBHW031156050726
47495CB00019B/2305